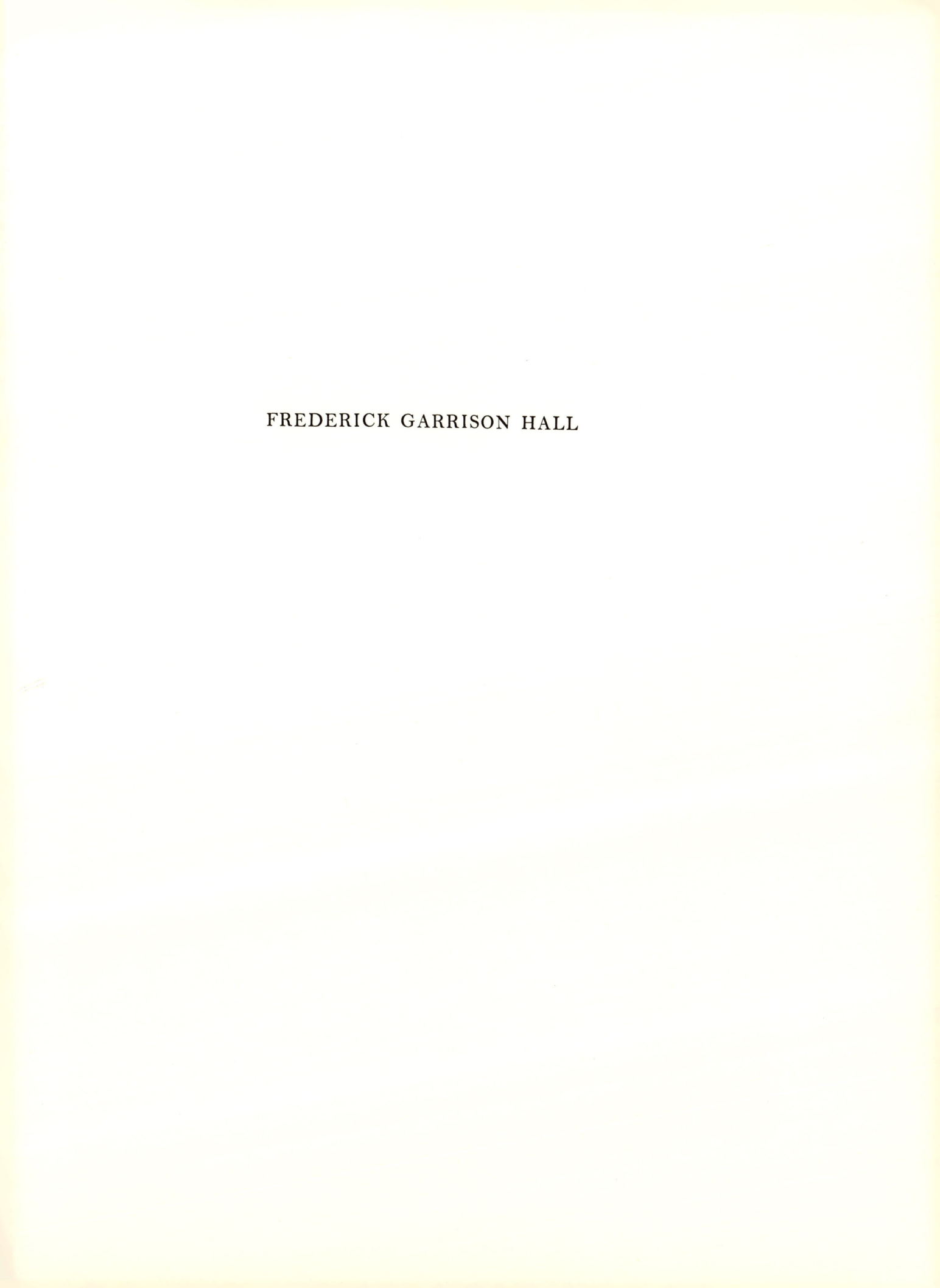

FREDERICK GARRISON HALL

FREDERICK GARRISON HALL
ETCHINGS · BOOKPLATES · DESIGNS

WITH A BIOGRAPHICAL SKETCH BY ARIEL HALL &
A PERSONAL MEMOIR BY HENRY P. ROSSITER

BY ELTON WAYLAND HALL
BOSTON · BOSTON PUBLIC LIBRARY · 1972

COPYRIGHT © 1972 BY ELTON WAYLAND HALL
LIBRARY OF CONGRESS CATALOGUE CARD NO. 72-86025

CONTENTS

7 Introduction
by Elton Wayland Hall

10 Frederick Garrison Hall
by Ariel Hall

13 Some Personal Memories of Freddy Hall
by Henry P. Rossiter

17 Etchings

83 Bookplates

99 Representative Drawings, Cover Designs, and Paintings

111 Bibliography

113 APPENDIX A
The Etchings of Frederick Garrison Hall
by Arthur W. Heintzelman

115 APPENDIX B
The Etchings of Frederick Garrison Hall
by Ameen Rihani

118 APPENDIX C
The Little People of F. G. Hall
by Ralph Bergengren

122 APPENDIX D
Catalogue of the Memorial Exhibition

127 Index of Prints

127 Index of Bookplates

129 General Index

FREDERICK GARRISON HALL
(Oil by Leslie P. Thompson, in the collection of the National Academy of Design)

INTRODUCTION

THE idea for this book was originated several years ago by Garrison K. Hall, a nephew of the artist, as a way to provide the various members of the family with a complete record of the etched work of Frederick Garrison Hall. At this time, there exists no complete set of his prints.

A major effort has been made to locate an impression of every etching he did for reproduction here, yet two titles listed in the March 1921 number of *The Print Connoisseur* have not come to light: "The Entrance to Pennsylvania Station" and "Italian Villa." With these exceptions, the catalogue is believed to be complete.

As Arthur Heintzelman pointed out, it is unusual that an etcher should have gained such high recognition for so few plates. In group shows, Hall often took top honors among etchers whose published plates numbered the better part of one thousand, and who are still reasonably well known today. With the comparatively recent renewal of interest in American etching of that period, the work of many long-neglected printmakers is again being collected. This renewed interest in collecting will have little effect on the popularity of Hall's work, simply because there are very few of his prints available to be collected. It is most unusual for print dealers to have any of Hall's prints at all, not to mention a group large enough to stimulate general interest. The bulk of his work is presumed to be in unknown private hands.

Yet regardless of whether Hall's prints are ever actively sought by collectors, he will have a place in the history of American etching and in our cultural history, because the popularity of his prints documents the taste of the 1920's and the 1930's when he regularly exhibited at the St. Botolph Club, the Copley Society, the Guild of Boston Artists, and Doll & Richards, his Boston dealers. These exhibits were invariably accompanied by most enthusiastic reviews in the local newspapers. Nor was his popularity limited to Boston, for, as may be seen in the catalogue, he won prizes in Brooklyn, Philadelphia, and Chicago as well. His print "Eglise de St. Nicolas du Chardonnet" was selected from a large group of American etchings for the collection of the

Bibliothèque Nationale in Paris. The Royal Italian Committee on Arts Acquisition selected prints by Frederick G. Hall and Ernest D. Roth to represent American etching at the Uffizi Gallery in Florence.

As so often happens when enthusiasm for a project develops, the project grows. A number of Frederick Hall's bookplates were published in a book by Richard Clipston Sturgis in 1905. Since the book is now very scarce and many plates were done after its publication, it seemed a good idea to include as complete a set as could be assembled. While collecting bookplates is not as fashionable as it once was, it is a fascinating subject, for, generally speaking, the history of the bookplate is the history of design. That the Hall bookplates fit this idea is shown by the strong art nouveau feeling of his early plates. No claim is made as to the completeness of the group, save that all plates known to the Hall family have been included.

Both the etchings and in many cases the bookplates of Frederick Hall reveal his deep interest in and understanding of architecture. Although he had an architectural background, he never went into professional practice. However, in 1921 a war memorial was erected in Gloucester. The memorial consisted of a smaller-scale version of the statue of Joan of Arc by Anna Vaughn Hyatt Huntington on Riverside Drive in New York. Frederick Hall contributed the design for the base of Cape Anne granite for which he received an enthusiastic compliment from the sculptress.

While an undergraduate at Harvard, Freddy Hall drew a number of covers for the *Lampoon* and *The Bookman*, a journal published by Dodd, Mead, & Company. Because magazines tend to be ephemeral, an example of each is included here.

During his lifetime, Freddy Hall was known primarily as a painter, and it was in this medium that the bulk of his work was done. His still lifes and portraits were well known in the Boston area, and travelled around the country in large group shows. His paintings were frequently singled out for praise, and reproduced in reviews of the shows. The two paintings reproduced here serve to point out that there was this other side to his artistic work.

One of the great pleasures of preparing a book such as this is that it affords one an opportunity to correspond with many enthusiastic and helpful people. I wish to thank the many curators of prints and their staffs who have provided information on their holdings, and particularly those who have permitted reproduction of their material. Walter Muir Whitehill made many encouraging suggestions which have added greatly to the book, and permitted seven bookplates in the Boston Athenæum collection to be reproduced. Sinclair Hitchings and Paul Swenson have been a great help in providing information on the Hall collection at the Boston Public Library, which is the most complete in existence. Eleanor Sayre and Karin Peltz of the Museum of Fine Arts have also been most helpful in answering queries on F. G. Hall material in their collection. Especial thanks go to Henry P. Rossiter, an old friend of the artist, for his memoir and to Ariel Hall for her biographical sketch of her husband.

Freeman Keith of The Stinehour Press was responsible for the composition of this book and offered many helpful suggestions of a design and editorial nature. All other details of production have been in the hands of John Peckham of The Meriden Gravure Company, who was involved with the project several years before the present writer.

E.W.H.

FREDERICK GARRISON HALL

BOSTON, Massachusetts, was the home of Frederick Garrison Hall for most of his life. Baltimore, Maryland, was his birthplace on the twenty-second of April 1878. He was the son of Myra (Garrison) and Joseph Thomas Hall. The Hall family had established itself in Maryland near the close of the seventeenth century with the arrival on these shores of the young Reverend Henry Hall, who had been sent in 1698, during the reign of William and Mary, by the Lord Bishop of London, with letters to the Governor of Maryland. The well-researched Hall family tree holds in its branches the names of Duvall, Contee, and Garrison, as well as two Governors of Maryland: Josias Fendall and Joseph Kent.

Frederick Hall, or "Freddy" as he was called by his friends, came to Boston in early childhood, with his mother and a younger brother, Irving Kent. He attended private schools and entered Harvard University in 1899, where he spent the next five years. Architecture was his first interest, but he later transferred his studies to art. During the Harvard years he was an editor of Harvard's *Lampoon* and did many excellent covers for that publication. He also designed bookplates for several eminent Bostonians at the request of William Dana Orcutt, distinguished editor of The University Press in Cambridge. The bookplates have few equals in any century and earned an international reputation for Frederick Hall at an early age.

One of the most fascinating of these bookplates was designed for his friend William Paxton, who was a teacher of Freddy's and a leading light of the so-called "Boston" school of art. These Boston artists believed in the fundamentals of technique and in realism. Their goal was obviously to create paintings both beautifully executed and truthful to the subject. They must have been aware of the emerging talents of Picasso, Matisse, Bracque, and others, but they preferred to remain faithful to a much older tradition: that of the seventeenth-century Dutch masters.

During his formative years Freddy Hall also loved the theatre and music. He and his brother Irving gave much of their free time to studying music and attending concerts. In their later lives both sponsored chamber music groups and orchestras, and assisted various artists in their careers. Freddy's favorite instrument seems to have been the harp. The story is told that he once leaned over the orchestra pit at a musical show and asked the harpist if he would give him lessons. He owned a harp for several years and practiced seriously, studying with Mildred Dilling, the well-known concert harpist, and with Bernard Zighera, first harpist with the Boston Symphony. Later in life he became a friend of Harpo Marx, who commissioned two F. G. Hall paintings.

The theatre was another strong interest, which, I think, shows itself in some of his etchings, with their formalized foregrounds and the famous "little people" who animate the French architectural scenes. Roland Young, the British star of stage, screen, and television, was another particularly close friend, who always stayed with the Halls when in Boston. He, also, owned two of the F. G. Hall paintings as did playwright Alice Duer Miller.

The years 1909 to 1912 were spent largely in Paris, where Freddy studied at the Academie Julien. It was in France that he drew almost all the churches, houses, old doorways, and street scenes that were etched on copper many years later. Short trips to Italy, Holland, and England also provided subjects for his pencil. Most of the etchings were made during the years 1917 to 1930. One exception is the "Eglise de Notre Dame in Dijon" which was done in 1946 and dedicated to the great French etcher Charles Meryon, whose art Freddy admired and emulated. Many of these etchings received prizes when they were first exhibited: notably the Alice Brinton Gold Medal (Philadelphia 1927), the Logan prize (Chicago 1926), the Charles M. Lee prize (Philadelphia 1936), and the Sesnan Gold Medal (Philadelphia 1928).

In 1909 Frederick Hall married Evelyn Ames, daughter of Oliver Ames of North Easton, thirty-first Governor of Massachusetts. Evelyn was a gifted pianist, and the homes they maintained at 260 Beacon Street, Boston, and at Eastern Point, Gloucester, were often the scene of concerts by great artists or chamber groups. Evelyn Hall was a unique character who should be remembered here. After her death in 1940, friends wrote of her "rare" personality—"vivid, warm, generous, and inspiring" with "tremendous mental vitality, enthusiasm, and magnetism." Much of the social life of Boston and the North Shore during those years revolved around this couple and the brilliant atmosphere they provided.

Until his own tragic death on October 16, 1946, Freddy also maintained a studio in the artists' building at 30 Ipswich Street, Boston. Here he kept businessman's hours, perhaps stopping by, on his way home, at the St. Botolph Club on Commonwealth Avenue. He was a convivial, jolly, entertaining person who belonged to several clubs, including The Players and the Coffee House in New York and the Harvard Club of New York. He was also particularly happy to be elected an associate of The National Academy of Design. Here he was elected as a painter, whereas most of his previous honors had come from etching. He was married again, in 1943, to the writer of this article—Ariel Wellington Perry, a professional harpist, the daughter of Everett Inwood and Clara (Brigham) Perry of Attleboro, Massachusetts. The second Mrs. Frederick Hall was a graduate of Smith College, with degrees from the Sorbonne in Paris and the Curtis Institute in Philadelphia, and pursued an active musical career both before and after marriage. This marriage ended sadly in 1946 when Freddy was struck by an automobile and lived but a few days afterward.

His major works had been accomplished: the portraits, commissioned or otherwise; the still lifes for which he was most renowned. These had Chinese or English porcelains as their inspiration and were painted in a beautiful, timeless technique which Freddy knew would never be "out of style." They are relatively few in number, as he painted slowly and meticulously. The list of their owners, when the paintings were exhibited at a Memorial Show in the spring of 1947 at the Boston Museum of Fine Arts, reads like a Who's Who of Boston society, liberally sprinkled with theatrical names. Freddy has left something else of himself which should not be forgotten. These are two short films, one serious, the other a burlesque representing a day in the life of an etcher. These are now in the Wiggin Collection of the Boston Public Library. The burlesque version, in particular, reveals much of Frederick Hall's great sense of humor and his charm. Perhaps they also reveal something of his ever-willing desire to help others. Examples of his work are in the Uffizi Gallery, Florence, the Bibliothèque Nationale, Paris, the Print Department of The Library of Congress in Washington, the Art Institute of Chicago, and the Museum of Fine Arts, Boston, as well as in many private collections.

Frederick Hall had no children of his own, but he was fortunate in having many nieces and nephews. These have all distinguished themselves and continue the traditional Hall love for music and the arts. Freddy was always "Uncle Fido" to these children and inspired and encouraged them. Now his faithfulness to artistic ideals will continue to inspire their children and all those who love beautiful things.

ARIEL HALL

SOME PERSONAL MEMORIES OF FREDDY HALL

I FIRST met Frederick G. Hall many years ago when he came to the Department of Prints, in the Museum of Fine Arts, to show me a group of his most recent etchings. From this meeting there grew up a mutual liking and a respect for each other's opinions, even when conflicting.

One of Freddy's most engaging qualities was his quick and buoyant sense of humor, often taking a whimsical or capricious turn, as when, at one of our weekly lunches together at a Boston hotel, he said he would like to form a club with only the two of us as members, its purpose being to have lobster and mince pie at the same meal.

For the Museum's series of films showing various techniques of printmaking, in which Timothy Cole demonstrated wood engraving and Frank Benson, etching, Freddy was asked to do one of drypoint. At the same time, at his own request and expense, he went on to do a parody of his drypoint. He himself planned and carried out its action, and commented on all the procedures. The opening scene shows him riding a bicycle, gaily and briskly, towards his Gloucester studio. Once there he assembles his materials and tools, including a small axe, to emphasize, he remarks impishly, the darkest passages of drypoint. For the numerous proofs he pulled and discarded, the ink he supposedly squeezed from a tube was actually chocolate cream, which he tested and tasted with boyish zest.

One autumn evening before an audience he personally had invited, he showed both his films in the house of his friend William Endicott, Treasurer of the Museum of Fine Arts. The subject of his film was a full-length portrait of an attractive young woman, a relative of the family. Freddy said it gave him a most unpleasant twinge to cut into the plate for the purpose of adding or correcting some detail, especially as the correction usually involved cutting into the subject.

After the showing I said that judging by the grim look on William Endicott's face, art had received a setback, that the heavy black beard and moustache which covered his face gave him a more saturnine expression than ever, but Freddy thought not. Many people had expressed their pleasure at seeing the films and enjoyed the parody, he said. The mention of the Endicott hirsute adornment reminded Freddy of a family story. A young niece had come to visit the Endicotts, and while she was sitting on his knee, gazing intently at him, her mother, passing by, said, "Kiss your Uncle William, dear." "But where, Mother, where?" asked the child.

From conversations with Freddy it was clear that he found etching the most responsive of the printmaking techniques. He thought that it provided the artist with a most sensitive and subtle medium—one able to express his thought and imagination completely, once he took the trouble to master its technical vagaries and understand its range. Freddy had a great admiration for the distinguished practitioners of the past. He did not attempt to imitate them, but it pleased him to recognize their difficulties and how they overcame them. Occasionally he mentioned how much labor and thought one of his plates had required, but the final result never showed that he had the slightest trouble with his work. It seems so spontaneous. On the other hand, he worked carefully, too, and left nothing to chance.

Working himself on a very delicate scale, but still aware of the breadth of the medium, he attained success and recognition in the particular section of the field he made his own.

Possibly next to his art Freddy loved music. He learned to play the harp with skill and appreciation. Frequently he had Harpo Marx as a guest in his Gloucester home. One day his wife, a brilliant pianist and accomplished musician, sat down and played for Harpo, resting nearby. "That was from Brahms," she said. "What makes you think so, darling?" responded Harpo.

Once I admired the color of the blue silk shirts Freddy always wore. He said he liked the color because frequently it cheered him, and gave a brighter outlook on things when they were at sixes and sevens.

HENRY P. ROSSITER
Curator Emeritus, Department of Prints and Drawings,
Museum of Fine Arts, Boston

ETCHINGS

All measurements are in inches.
Height is indicated first, then width.

1. THE ROCKY FIELD
 4¾ by 7   Ca. 1918   Edition: 20
From an impression in the collection of the Boston Public Library.

2. SALEM CEDAR
9½ by 7½   Ca. 1918   Edition: 25
From an impression in the collection of Garrison K. Hall.

3. THE CAVE
    9½ by 7   Ca. 1918   Edition: 40
From an impression in the collection of Garrison K. Hall.
Another impression is in the collection of the Museum of Fine Arts, Boston.

4. OLD WILLOWS
7¼ by 8⅝   Ca. 1917   Edition: 50

From an impression in the collection of Garrison K. Hall.
Other impressions are in the collections of the Boston Public Library, Library of Congress, National Collection of Fine Arts, and Yale University Art Gallery.

5. BEACH AND WILLOWS
    7 by 10½   Ca. 1918   Edition: 50
From an impression in the collection of Garrison K. Hall.
Other impressions are in the collections of the Boston Public Library, Library of Congress, Museum of Fine Arts, Boston, and Yale University Art Gallery.

6. NILES POND
    8⅜ by 6⅝   Ca. 1919   Edition: 60
From an impression in the collection of Garrison K. Hall.
Other impressions are in the collections of the Boston Public Library and Library of Congress.

7. OLD WILLOW
  3 by 2⅝   Ca. 1919   Edition: 30
From an impression in the collection of Garrison K. Hall.
Another impression is in the collection of the Boston Public Library.

8. THE CLIFF
    4⅝ by 5¾   Ca. 1918   Edition: 40
From an impression in the collection of Garrison K. Hall.
Other impressions are in the collections of the Boston Public Library and Library of Congress.

[31]

9. BY THE POND
7¼ by 4¾   Ca. 1920   Edition: 100 signed proofs

Frontispiece to the March 1921 number of *The Print Connoisseur*.
From an impression in the collection of the Boston Public Library.
Other impressions are in the collections of the Museum of Fine Arts, Boston, and New York Public Library.

10. THE DESERTED SHIPYARD
6¾ by 6⅛   Ca. 1920   Edition: 60
From an impression in the collection of Garrison K. Hall.
Another impression is in the collection of the Boston Public Library.

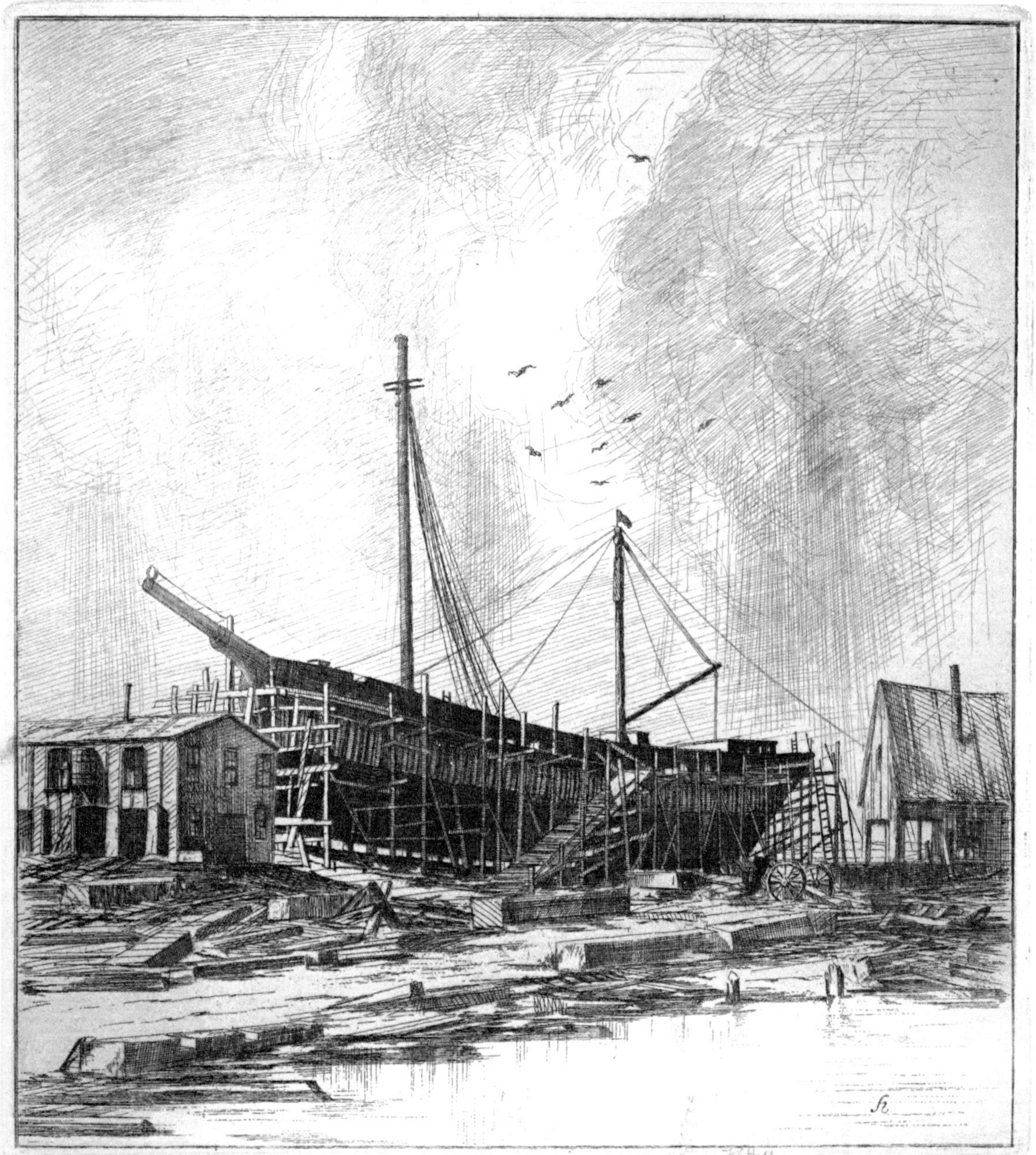

11. LA PENSIONNAIRE AMERICAINE
11¾ by 7⅞   Ca. 1920   Edition: 40
From an impression in the collection of The Library of Congress.

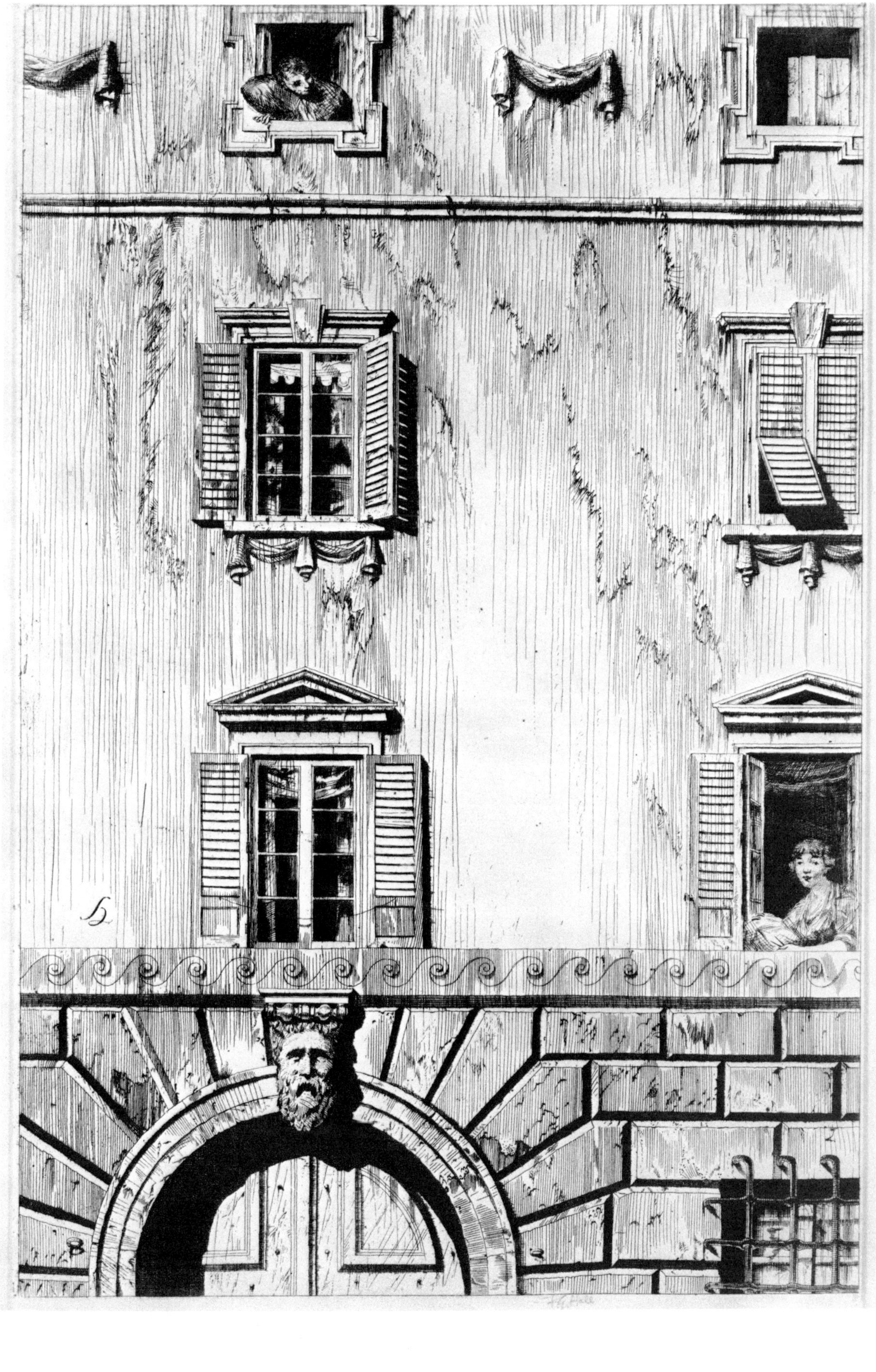

12. BOSTON PUBLIC LIBRARY
14¾ by 7⅛   1919   Edition: 50
From an impression in the collection of Garrison K. Hall.
Another impression is in the collection of the Boston Public Library.

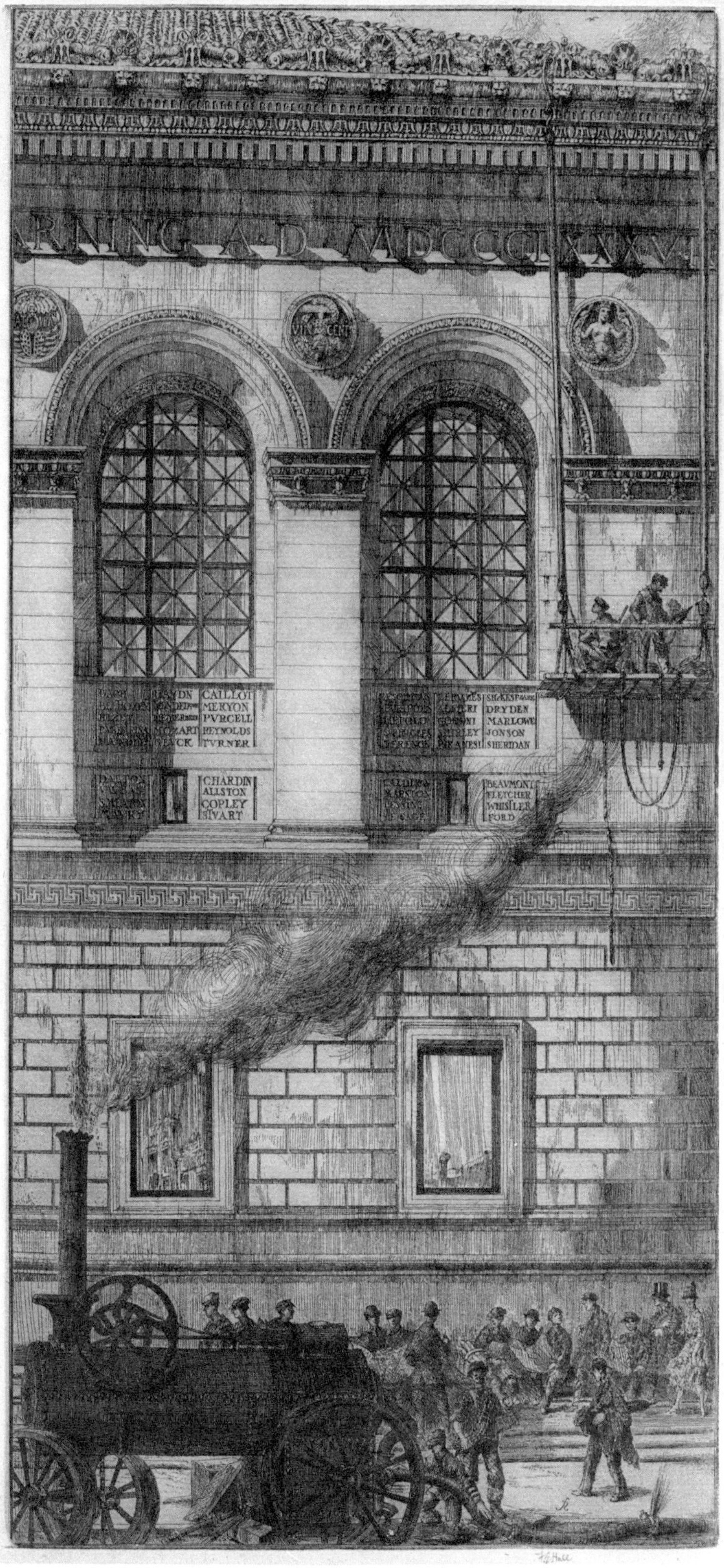

13. HOUSE IN VICENZA
    8⅜ by 6⅜   1920   Edition: 60
From an impression in the collection of Garrison K. Hall.
Nathan I. Bijur Prize, Brooklyn Society of Etchers, 1920.
Other impressions are in the collections of the Boston Public Library and Cleveland Museum of Art.

[41]

14. OLD HOUSES ON THE TIBER
    10 by 11⅝   Ca. 1920   Edition: 60

From an impression in the collection of Garrison K. Hall.
Alice McFadden Eyre Gold Medal, Pennsylvania Academy of the Fine Arts, 1927.
Jennie Sesnan Gold Medal, Philadelphia, 1928.
Other impressions are in the collections of the Boston Public Library, Cleveland Museum of Art, Library of Congress, National Collection of Fine Arts, and Philadelphia Museum.

15. ITALIAN VILLA
    Before March 1921   Edition: 40

No impression located.

16. ENTRANCE TO PENNSYLVANIA STATION
    Before March 1921   Edition: 60

No impression located.

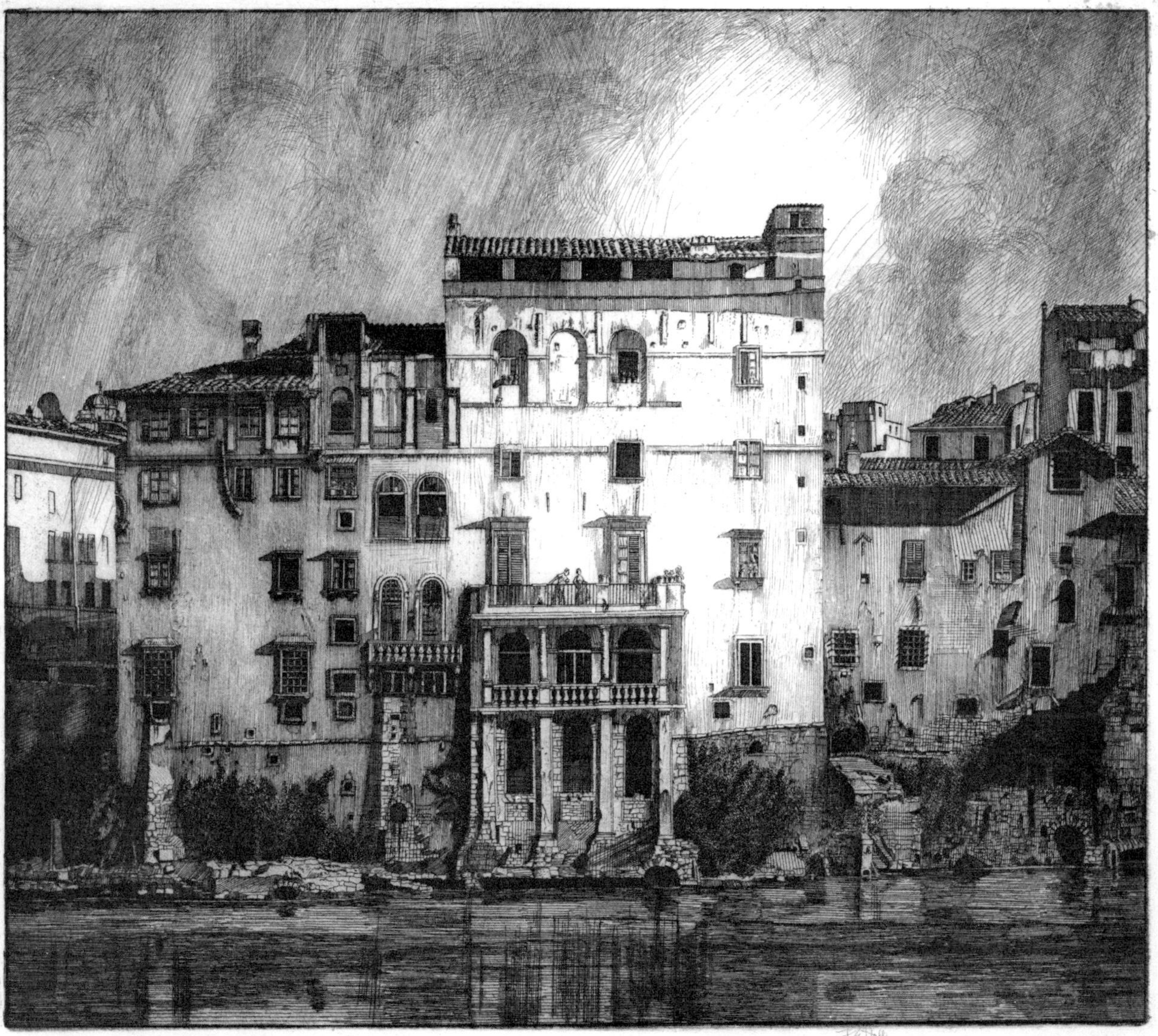

17. HOUSE IN OLERON
    11⅝ by 7⅞   Ca. 1921   Edition: 75

From an impression in the collection of the Boston Public Library.
Other impressions are in the collections of the Cleveland Museum of Art and Library of Congress.

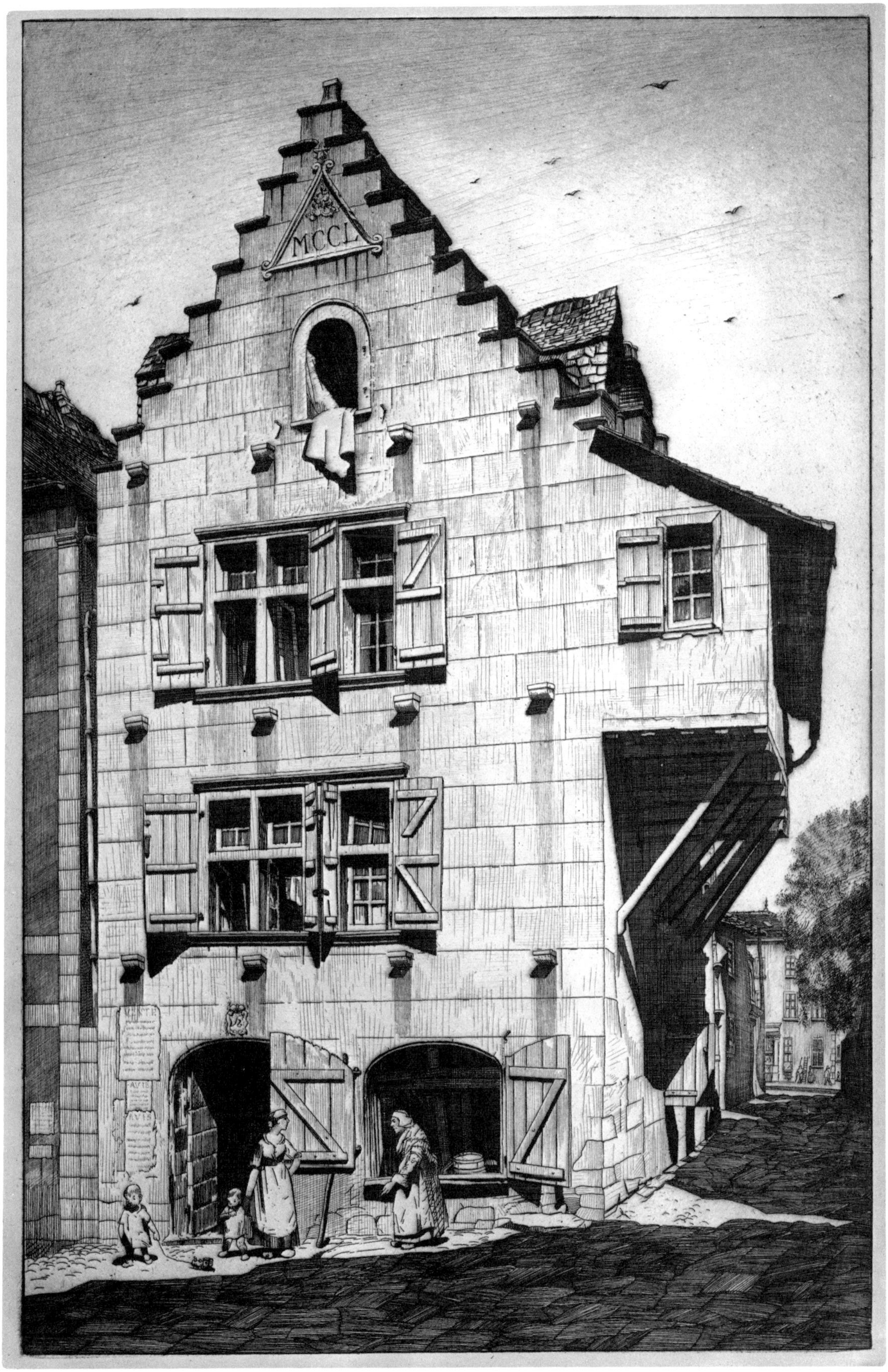
MCCL

18. ANCIENT DOORWAY, NEVERS
8¾ by 6⅛   Ca. 1921   Edition: 75

From an impression in the collection of Garrison K. Hall.
Other impressions are in the collections of the Boston Public Library, Cleveland Museum of Art, and National Collection of Fine Arts.

[47]

19. OLD FRENCH HALF-TIMBERED HOUSES, LE MANS
11¾ by 8⅝   Ca. 1922   Edition: 75

From an impression in the collection of the Boston Public Library.

Other impressions are in the collections of the Cleveland Museum of Art, Fogg Art Museum, Museum of Fine Arts, Boston, and Philadelphia Museum of Art.

[49]

20. HOTEL MORET
    8 by 5⅞   Ca. 1922   Edition: 75
From an impression in the collection of Garrison K. Hall.
Other impressions are in the collections of the Boston Public Library, Cleveland Museum of Art, and Library of Congress.

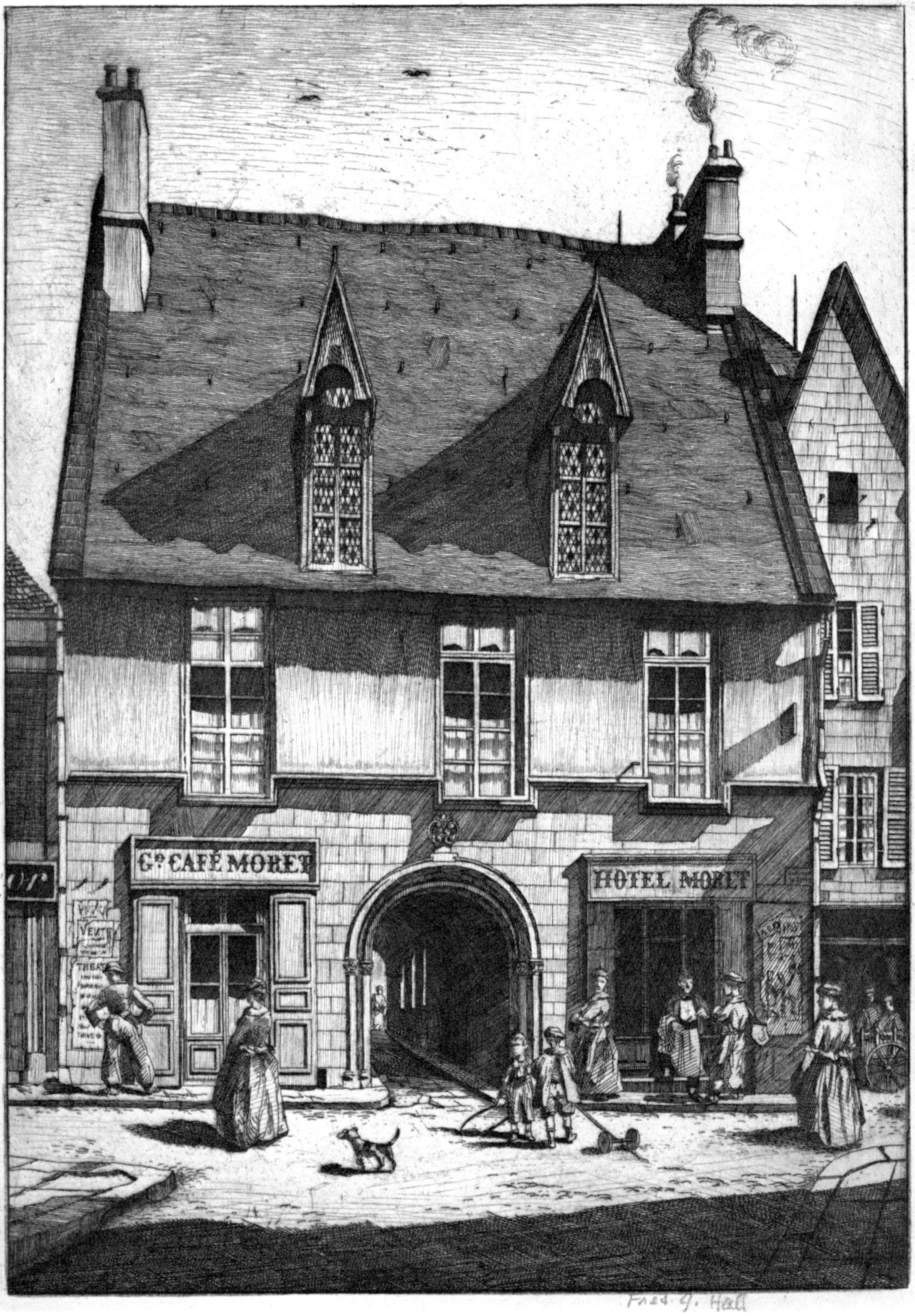
Gd CAFÉ MORET
HOTEL MORET
Fred G. Hall

21. HOUSE IN NANTES
13⅛ by 9¾   Ca. 1923   Edition: 75
From an impression in the collection of Garrison K. Hall.
Other impressions are in the collections of The Art Institute of Chicago, Boston Public Library, Museum of Fine Arts, Boston, and National Collection of Fine Arts.

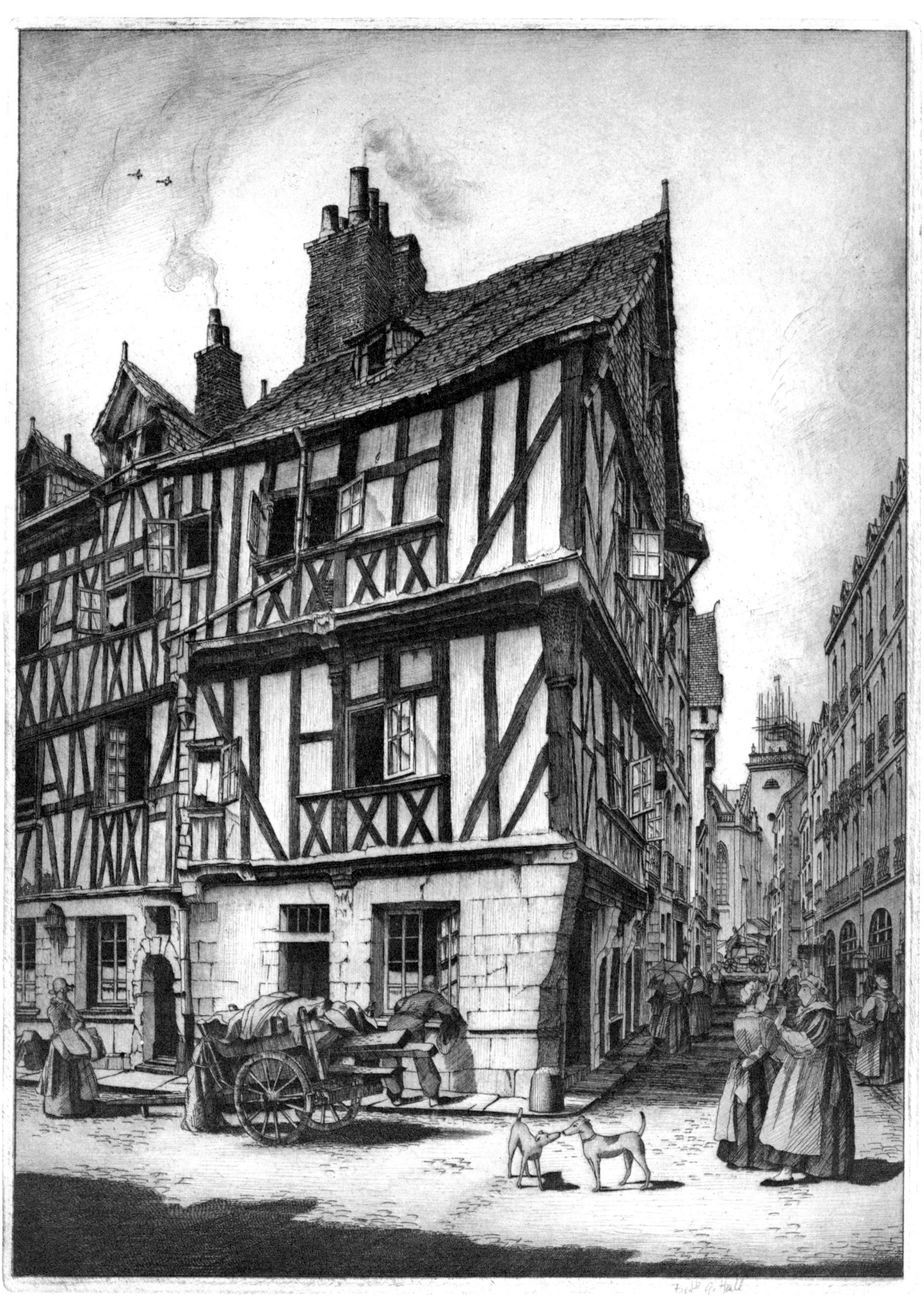

22. OLD TIMER
11⅞ by 8   Ca. 1923   Edition: 75
From an impression in the collection of Garrison K. Hall.
Another impression is in the collection of the Boston Public Library.

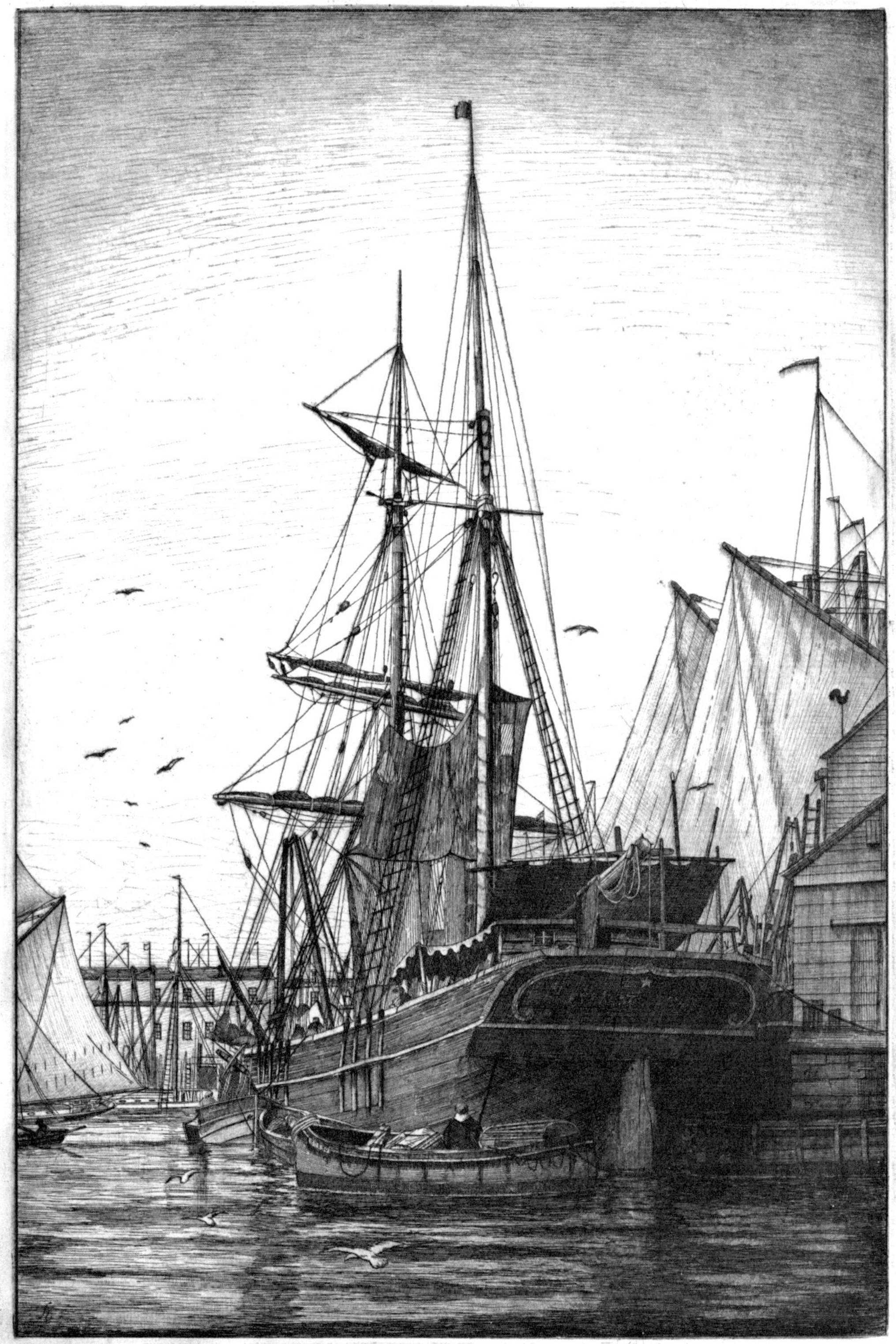

23. MAISON DES AMBASSADEURS, DIJON
13⅞ by 9¾   1924   Edition: 75

From an impression in the collection of Garrison K. Hall.
Silver Medal, Sesqui-centennial International Exposition, Philadelphia, 1926.
Other impressions are in the collections of the Boston Public Library, Fogg Art Museum, Museum of Fine Arts, Boston, National Collection of Fine Arts, and Uffizi Gallery. The copper plate is in the collection of the Boston Public Library.

[57]

24. EGLISE DE ST. NICOLAS DU
    CHARDONNET
    13¾ by 11⅛   1925   Edition: 75
From an impression in the collection of Garrison K. Hall.
Honorable Mention, Philadelphia Print Club, 1925.

Other impressions are in the collections of the Bibliothèque Nationale, Paris, Boston Public Library, Cleveland Museum of Art, Museum of Fine Arts, Boston, National Collection of Fine Arts, and New York Public Library.

Eglise de
S.t Nicolas du Chardonnet

25. LA MAISON DES CARIATIDES, DIJON
17 by 9⅜   1925   Edition: 75

From an impression in the collection of Garrison K. Hall.
Charles M. Lea Prize, Philadelphia Print Club, 1926.
Logan Prize, Chicago Society of Etchers, 1926.
Other impressions are in the collections of The Art Institute of Chicago, Boston Public Library, Cleveland Museum of Art, Library of Congress, National Collection of Fine Arts, and Philadelphia Museum of Art. The copper plate is in the collection of the Boston Public Library.

ANTIQUITÉS
AUX ANCÊTRES
CURIOSITÉS
LA MAISON DES CARIATIDES
DIJON

26. TOUR GOGUIN
   12¾ by 10⅜   1926   Edition: 75
From an impression in the collection of the Boston Public Library.
Reproduced in *Fine Prints of the Year*, 1927.
Another impression is in the collection of the Museum of Fine Arts, Boston.

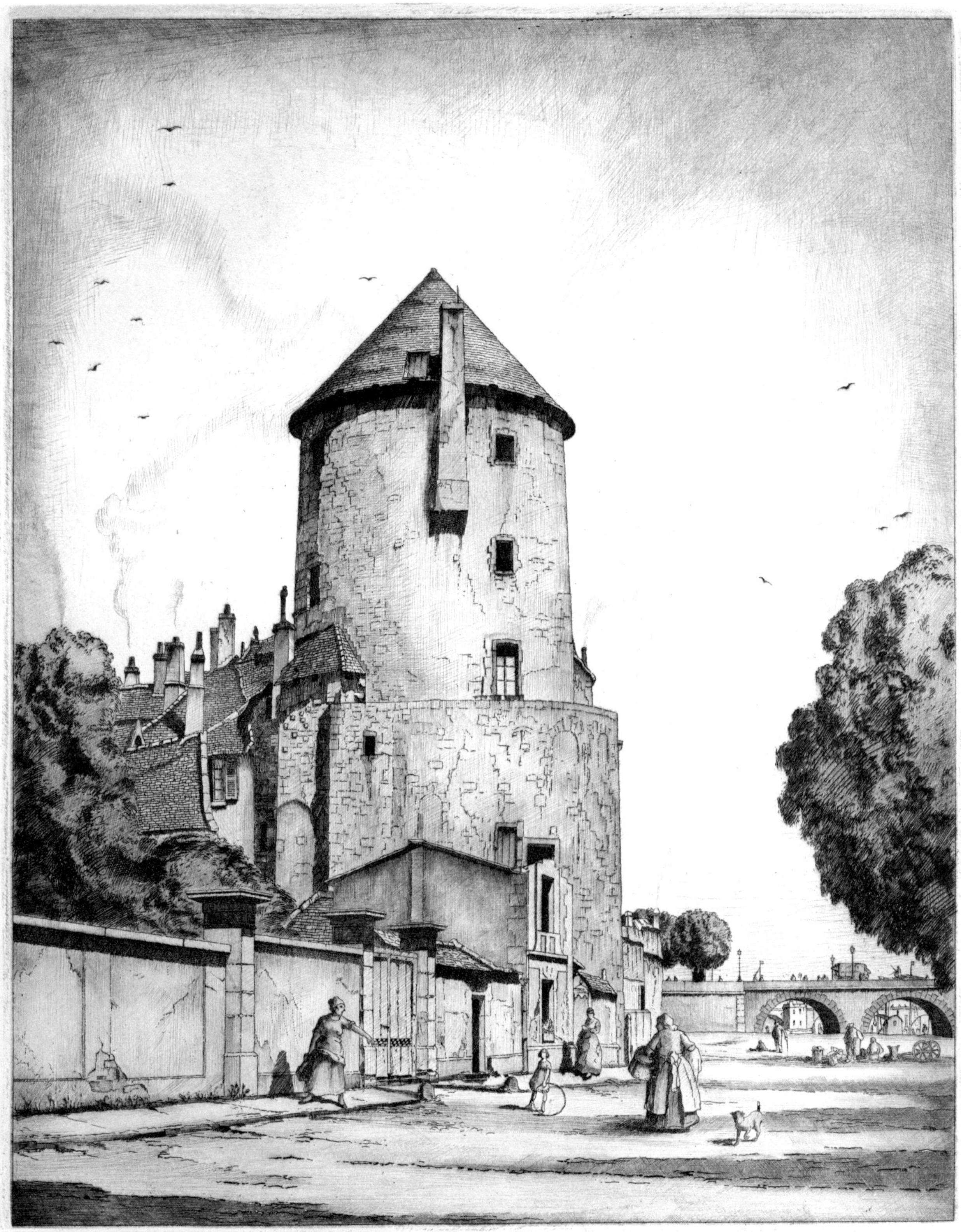

27. LITTLE FRENCH MARKET
    12⅛ by 8⅝   1926   Edition: 75

From an impression in the collection of Garrison K. Hall.
Alice Brinton Gold Medal, Philadelphia Print Club, 1927.
Reproduced in *Fine Prints of the Year*, 1926.

Other impressions are in the collections of the Boston Public Library, Cleveland Museum of Art, National Collection of Fine Arts, and New York Public Library. The copper plate is in the collection of the Boston Public Library.

Gd CHANTIER DU VAL DE GRACE
BOIS & CHARBONS
AU COURS des HALLES
BAR
160

28. A SCENE IN TOURS
   12⅝ by 8⅛   1927   Edition: 75

From an impression in the collection of Garrison K. Hall.
Honorable Mention, Philadelphia Print Club, 1927.
Other impressions are in the collections of the Boston Public Library, Fogg Art Museum, and National Collection of Fine Arts. The copper plate is in the collection of the Boston Public Library.

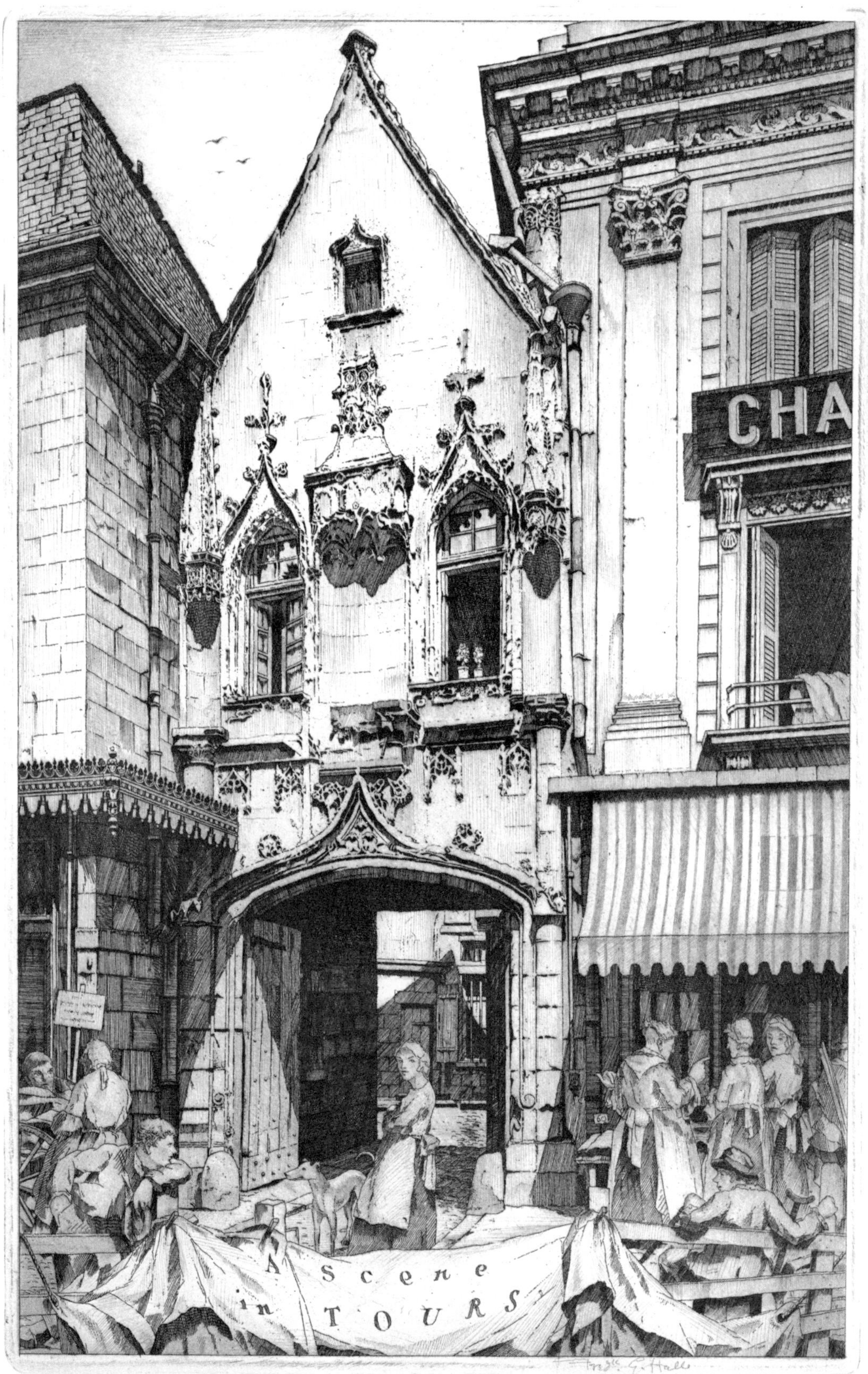
CHA
A Scene in TOURS

29. ROUEN, PORTE DE GUILLAUME
14⅜ by 11⅛   1928   Edition: 75

From an impression in the collection of Garrison K. Hall.
Reproduced in *Fine Prints of the Year*, 1928.
Other impressions are in the collections of The Art Institute of Chicago, Boston Public Library, Library of Congress, Museum of Fine Arts, Boston, and National Collection of Fine Arts. The copper plate is in the collection of the Boston Public Library.

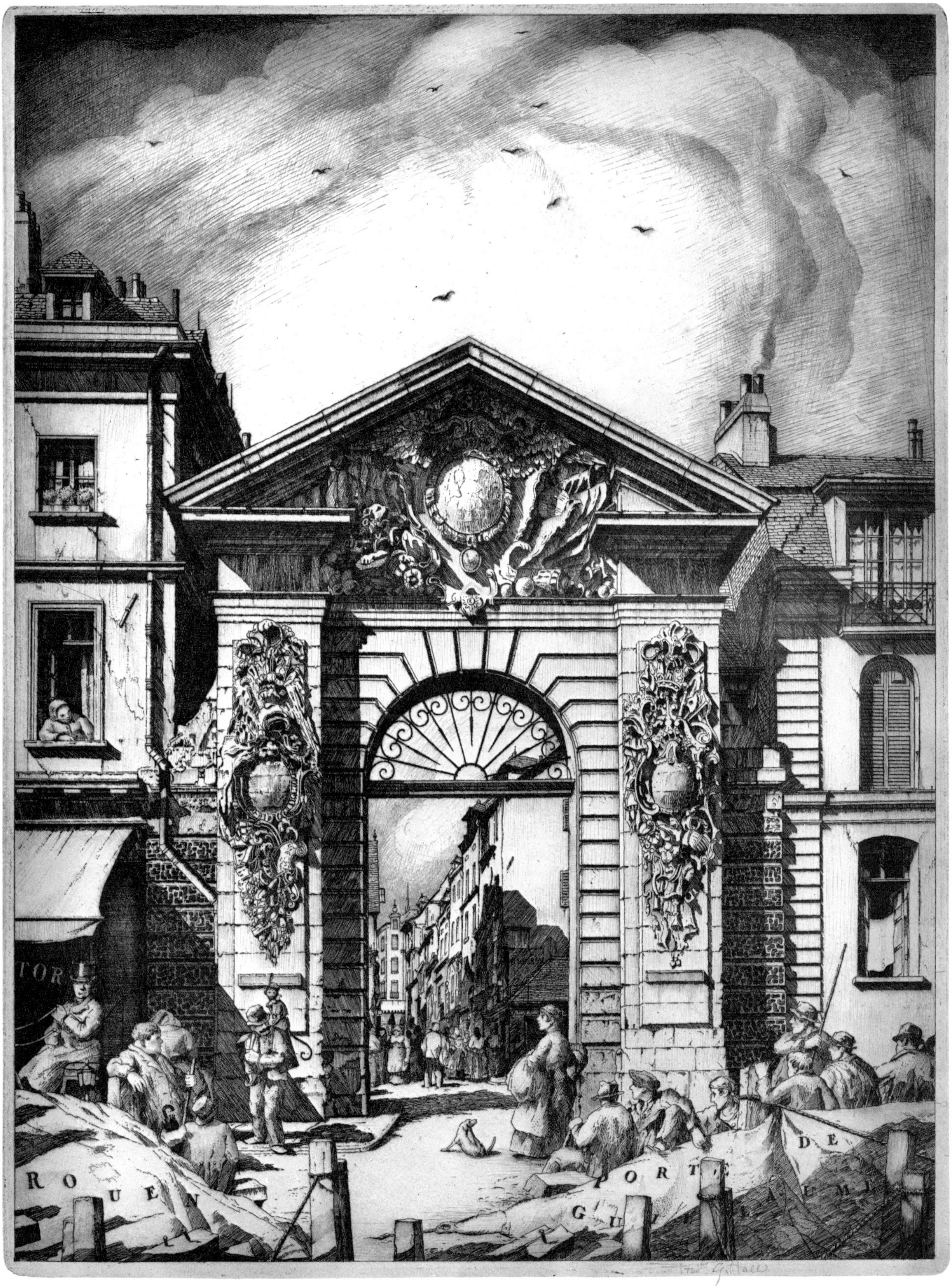

ROUEN
PORTE DE GUILLAUME

30. GATEWAY, ROTTERDAM
13½ by 10⅞   1929   Edition: 75

From an impression in the collection of Garrison K. Hall.

Other impressions are in the collections of the Boston Public Library, Museum of Fine Arts, Boston, National Collection of Fine Arts, and New York Public Library.

[71]

31. DIJON, EGLISE DE NOTRE DAME
    16¾ by 9⅞   1946   Edition unknown
An impression is in the collection of the Boston Public Library.
Not reproduced.

32. DIJON, EGLISE DE NOTRE DAME
    15¾ by 9⅜   1946   Second plate, second state of three
From an impression in the collection of the Boston Public Library.
An impression of each state is in the collection of the Boston Public Library.

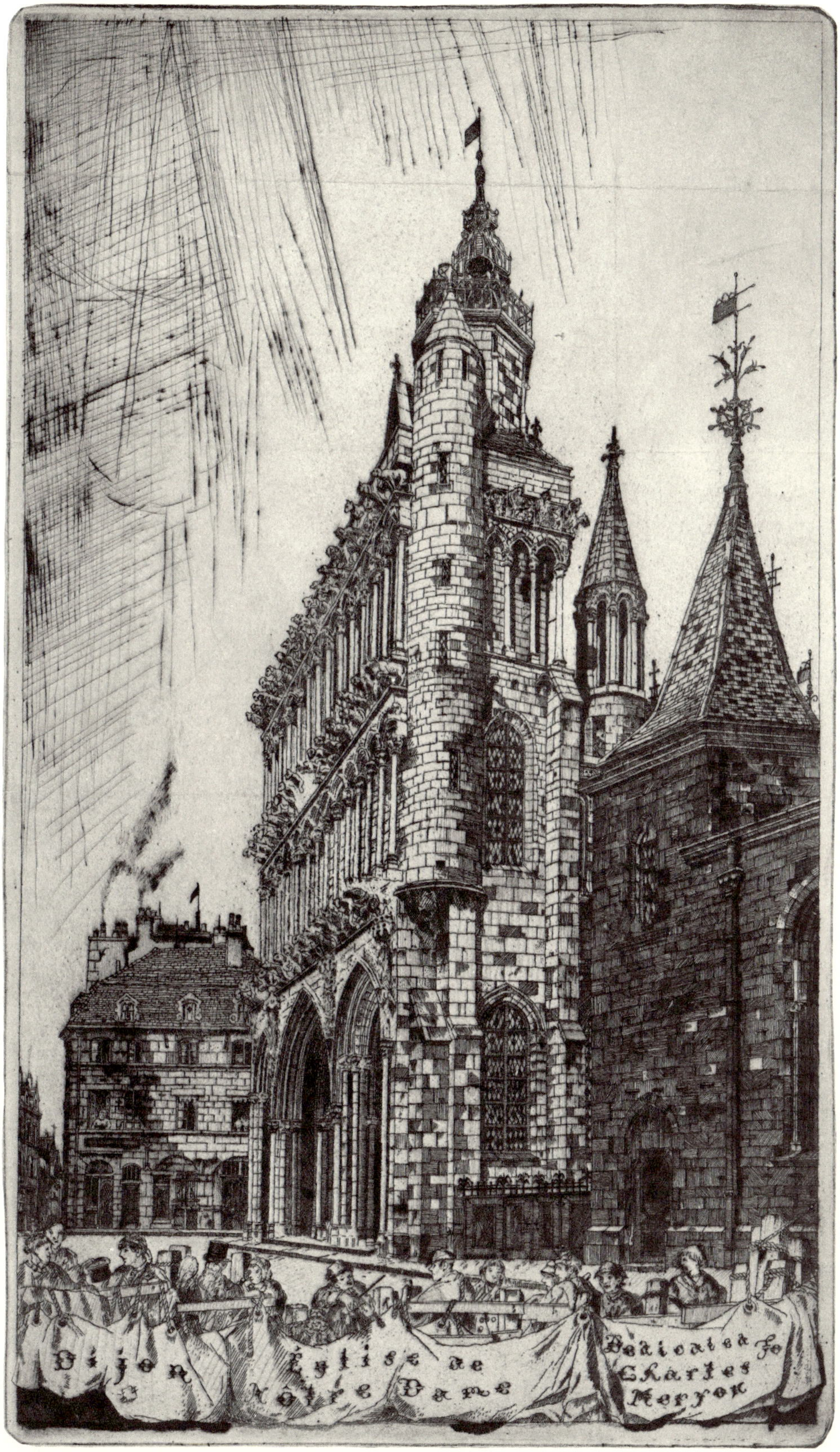
Dijon
Église de Nôtre Dame
Dedicated to Charles Meryon

33. DIJON, EGLISE DE NOTRE DAME
15⅛ by 9¼   1946   Third plate, fifth state of five
Edition: 60

From an impression in the collection of Garrison K. Hall.
An impression of each state is in the collection of the Boston Public Library, and an impression of one state is in the collection of the Museum of Fine Arts, Boston.

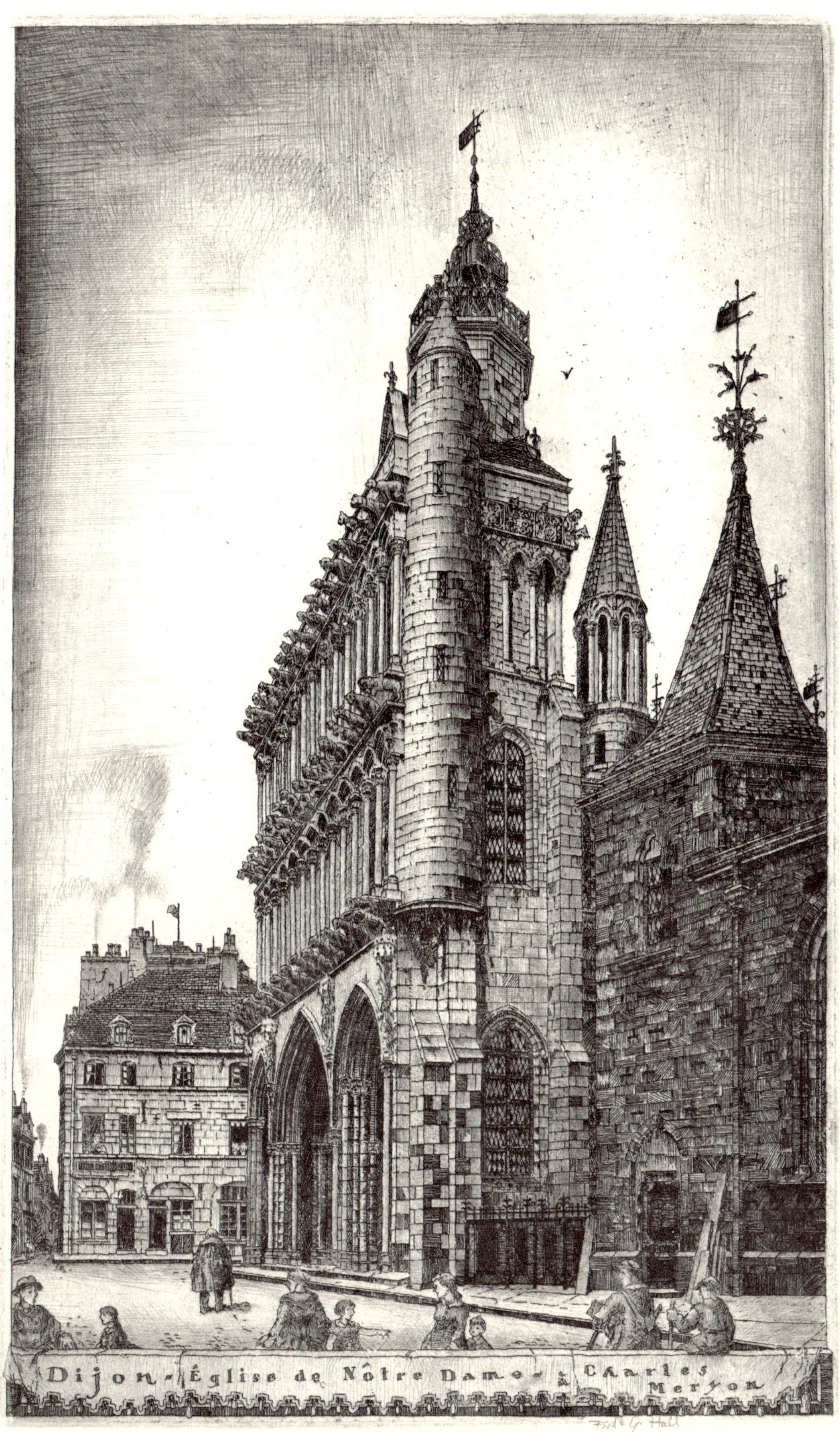
Dijon - Église de Nôtre Dame - à Charles Meryon

34. DIANA
   6⅜ by 5¼   1929   Edition: 40
From an impression in the collection of Garrison K. Hall.
Other impressions are in the collections of the Boston Public Library, Fogg Art Museum, and Museum of Fine Arts, Boston.

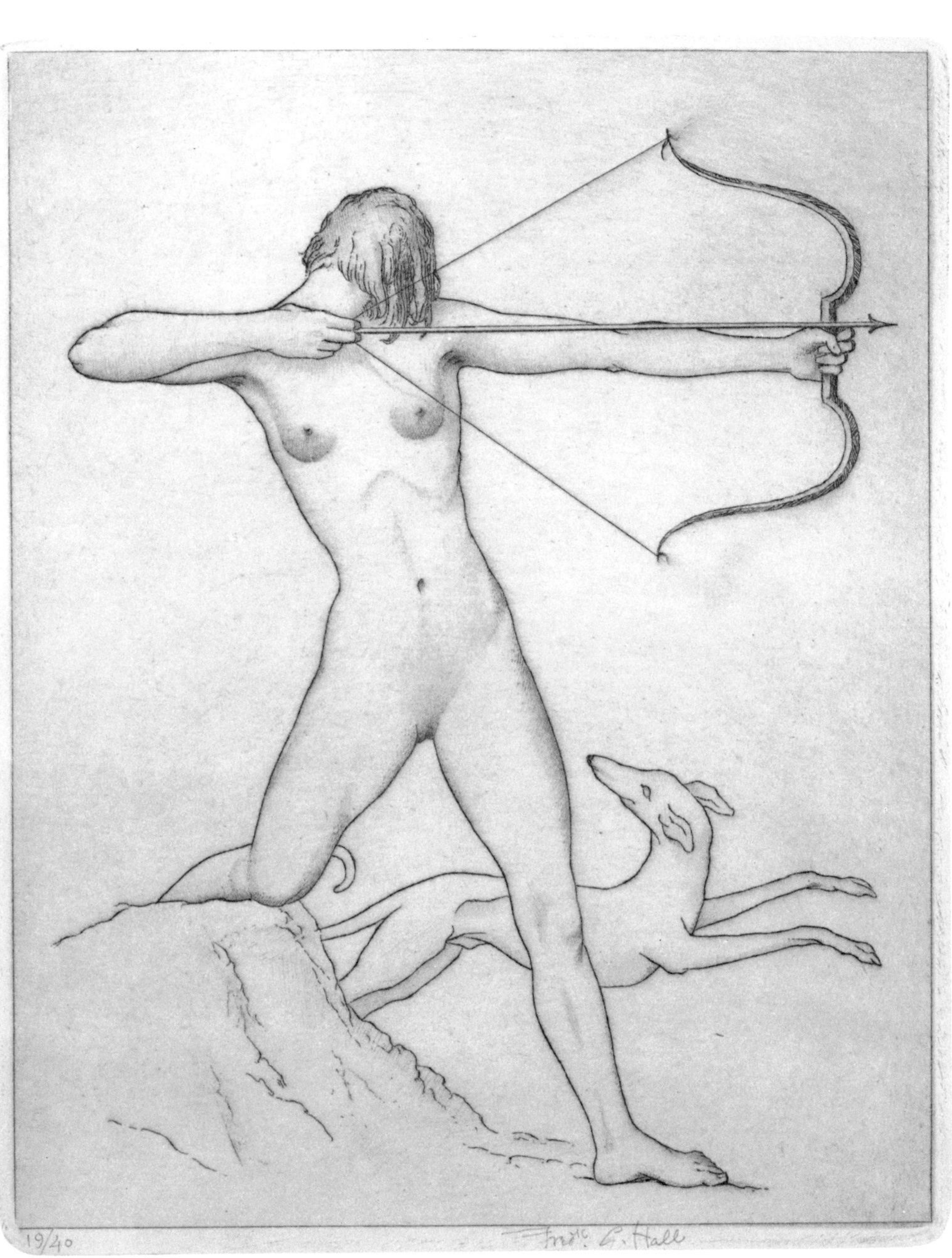
19/40
Fred^c G. Hall

35. MRS. CHARLES J. PRESCOTT, JR.
Drypoint   11¾ by 8¼   1929
From an impression in the collection of the Museum of Fine Arts, Boston.
This print was made for a movie on the drypoint process, one of a series produced by the Museum of Fine Arts. The subject is a cousin of the artist.

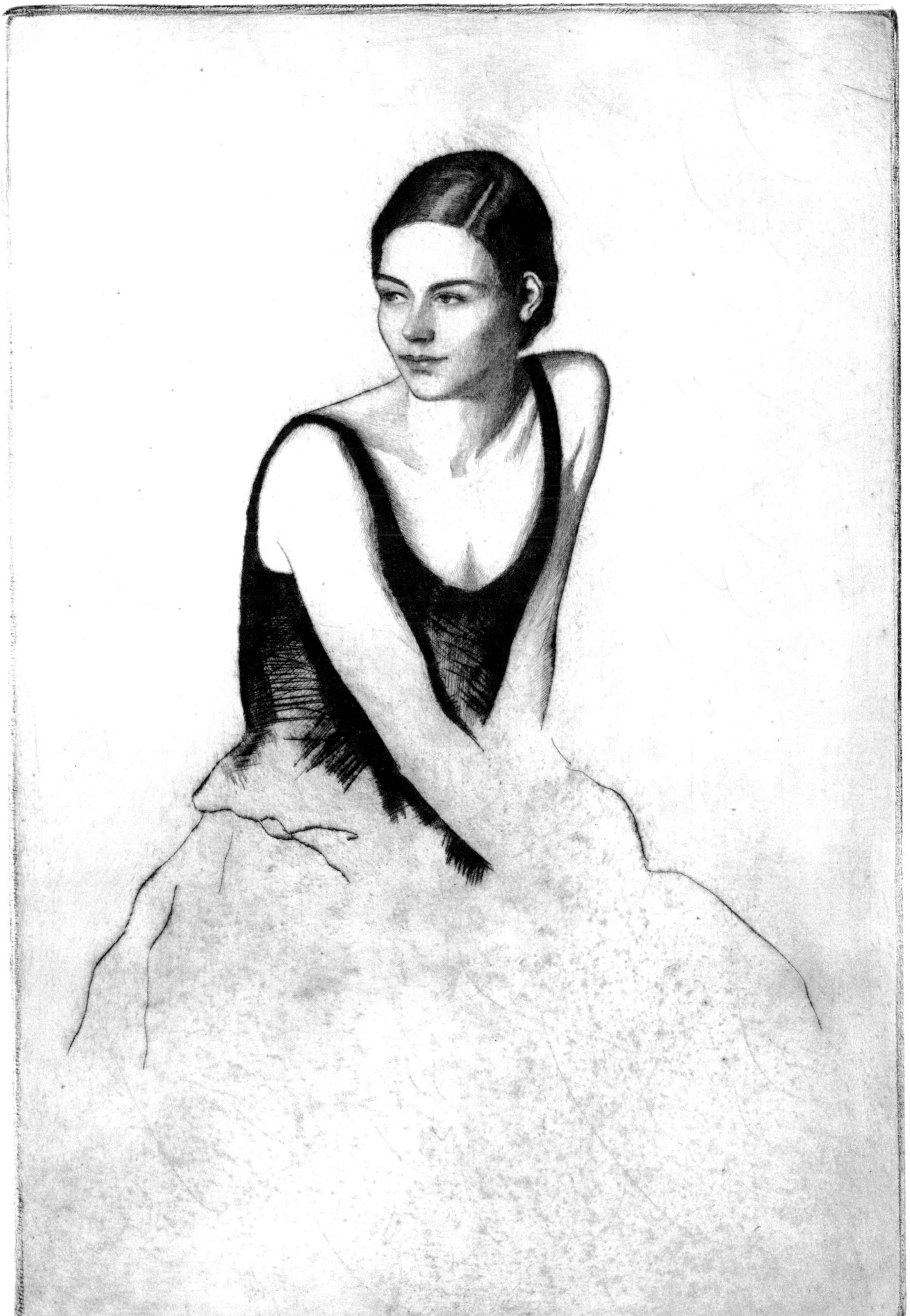

FREDERICK GARRISON HALL
1929

BOOKPLATES

Note: The bookplates were produced between the years 1901 and 1919, and many of them are dated. They were generally photomechanically reproduced from drawings, and some of them seem to have gone through more than one printing, which would account for slight variations in size between different impressions of the same bookplate. They are reproduced here at actual size and are arranged alphabetically by owner as a visual checklist.

[83]

[84]

[85]

[86]

[87]

IRVING KENT HALL
HELEN MACY HALL
Ex Libris
1912

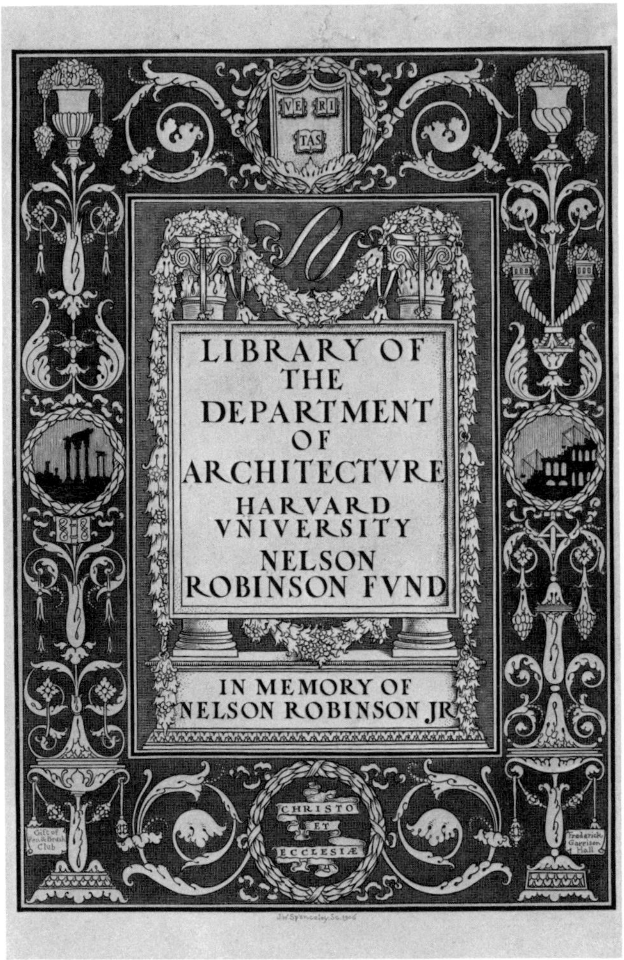
VE RI TAS
LIBRARY OF THE DEPARTMENT OF ARCHITECTVRE
HARVARD VNIVERSITY
NELSON ROBINSON FVND
IN MEMORY OF NELSON ROBINSON JR
CHRISTO ET ECCLESIAE

ALISON
HAUGHTON
EXLIBRIS
H
1904

PARKER·MORSE·HOOPER
HIS BOOK

ISAAC
JACKSON
EX
LIBRIS

Lillian Durham Jones
Ex Libris

JOSEPH DE FOREST
JUNKIN, JR
RARE BOOKS
EX LIBRIS
Frederick G. Hall

EX LIBRIS
KATHARINE
WARD
LANE

CLARENCE
COOK
LITTLE
EX
LIBRIS
1906

SUSAN M
LORING
EX LIBRIS

WILLIAM CALEB LORING
EX LIBRIS

LAWRENCE
MOTT
EX LIBRIS

[91]

ZIJN BOEK
HERMAN
CHRISTIAAN
JVRIAAN
ROELVINK

ARMIN
·A·
SCHLESINGER
His
Book

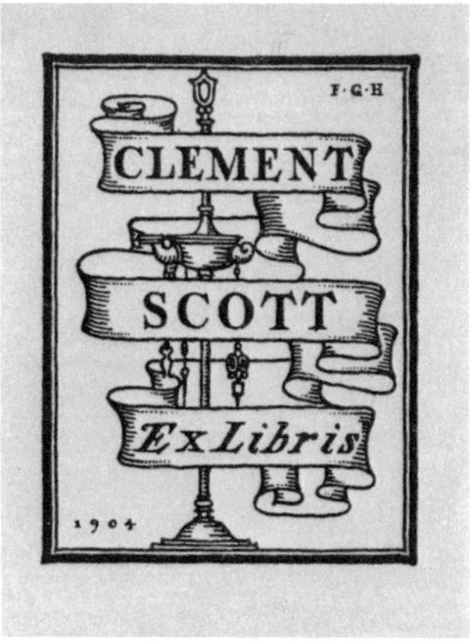
F·G·H
CLEMENT
SCOTT
Ex Libris
1904

ELEANOR
COCHRANE
SEARS
Ex
LIBRIS

[93]

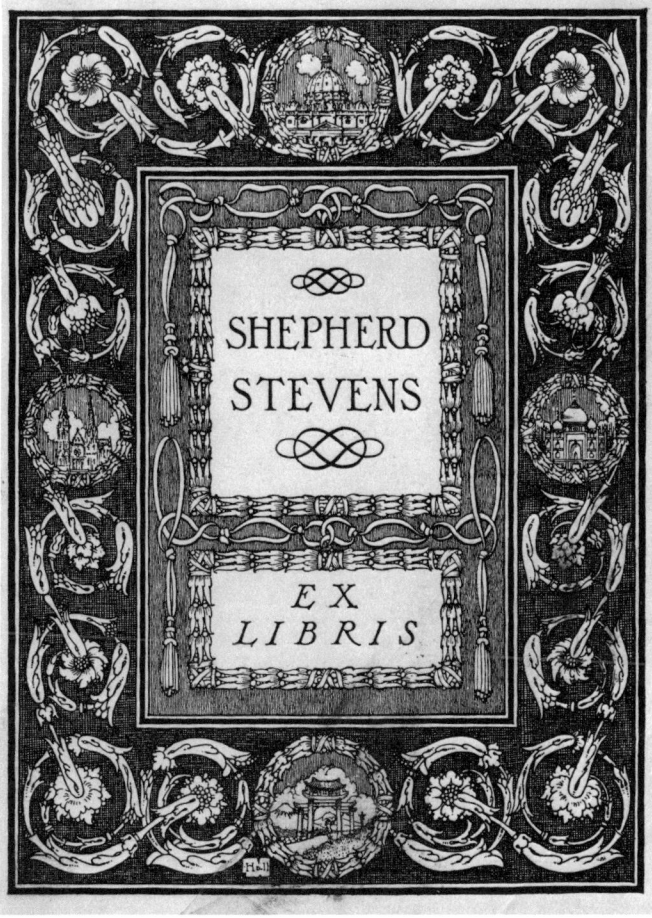

HERBERT NATHAN STRAVS
EX LIBRIS

EX LIBRIS RICHARD CLIPSTON STURGIS·JR

AMY IVERS TRVESDELL
HER BOOK

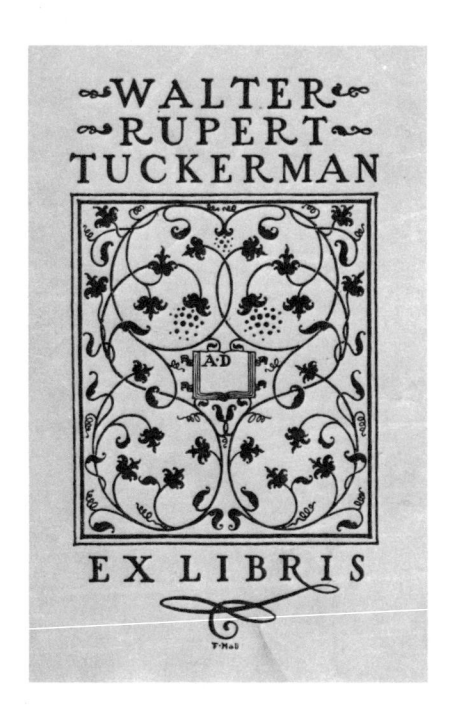

WALTER RUPERT TUCKERMAN
EX LIBRIS

[94]

[95]

REPRESENTATIVE DRAWINGS, COVER DESIGNS, AND PAINTINGS

CHURCH OF ST. MARY WOOLNOTH, LONDON
Pencil drawing   14 by 9⅜   1928
In the collection of the Boston Public Library.

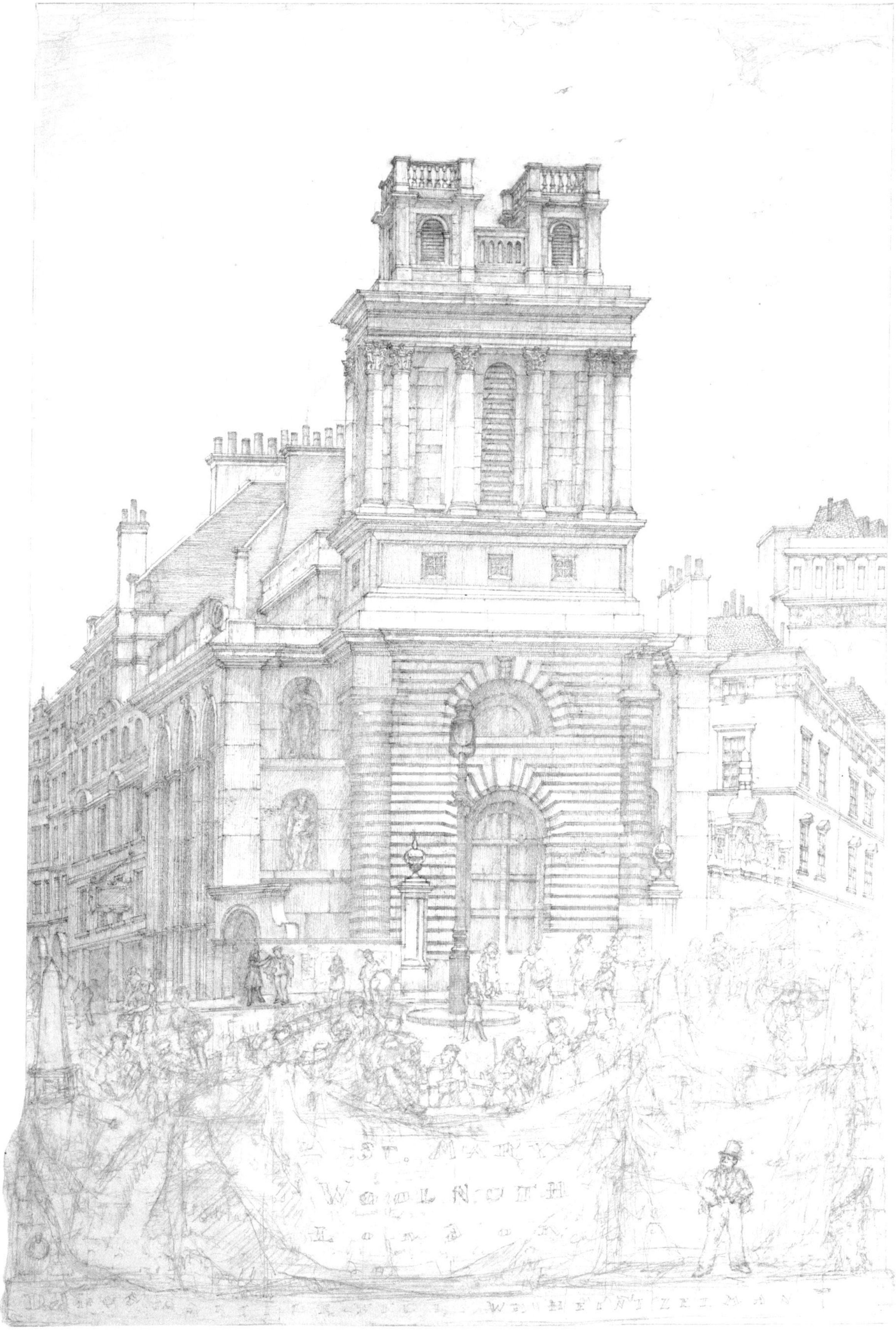
ST. MARY
WOOLNOTH
LONDON

HEAD OF A GIRL
Pencil drawing   11 9/16 by 9 1/16
In the collection of Elton W. Hall.

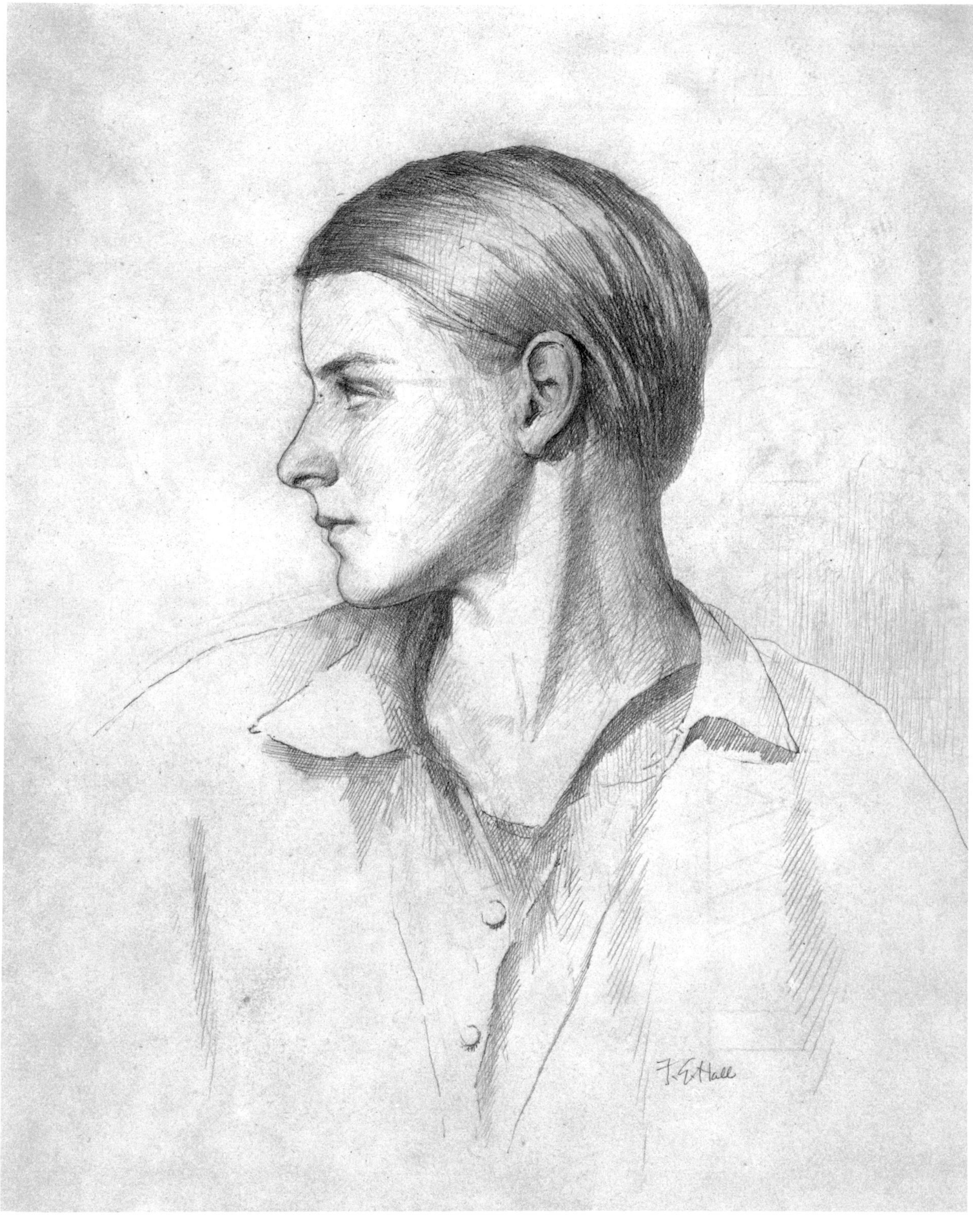
J. E. Hall

Cover for Harvard *Lampoon*, Christmas 1901
10 by 8⅛

THE HARVARD LAMPOON

CHRISTMAS NVMBER
MCMI

Cover for *The Bookman*, October 1902
9 13/16 by 6 3/4

Vol. XVI. OCTOBER, 1902 No. 2.

The BOOKMAN
October Number
Fully Illustrated

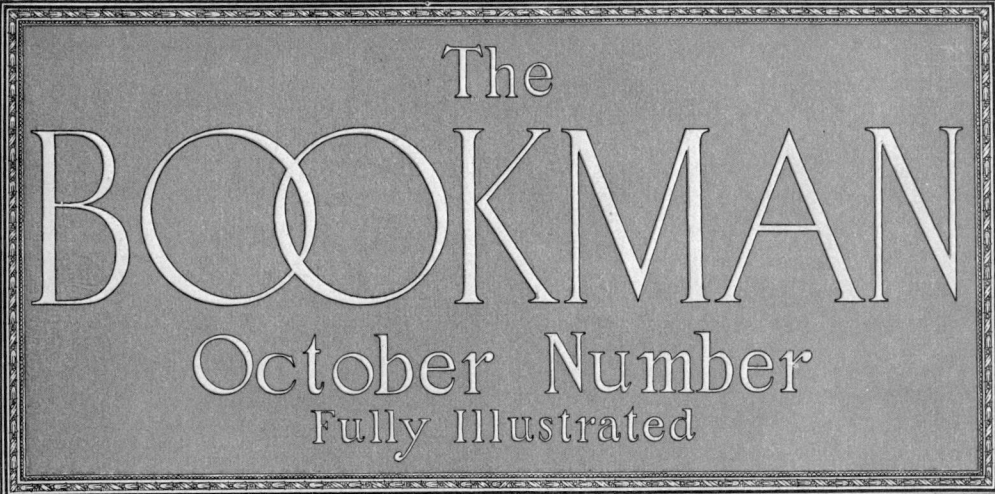

I AM A BOOKMAN — James Russell Lowell

DODD MEAD AND COMPANY

Price Twenty Five Cents Two Dollars per Year

TWO WHITE BIRDS
Oil on panel   30¼ by 25¼
In the collection of Mrs. J. Henry Fair.

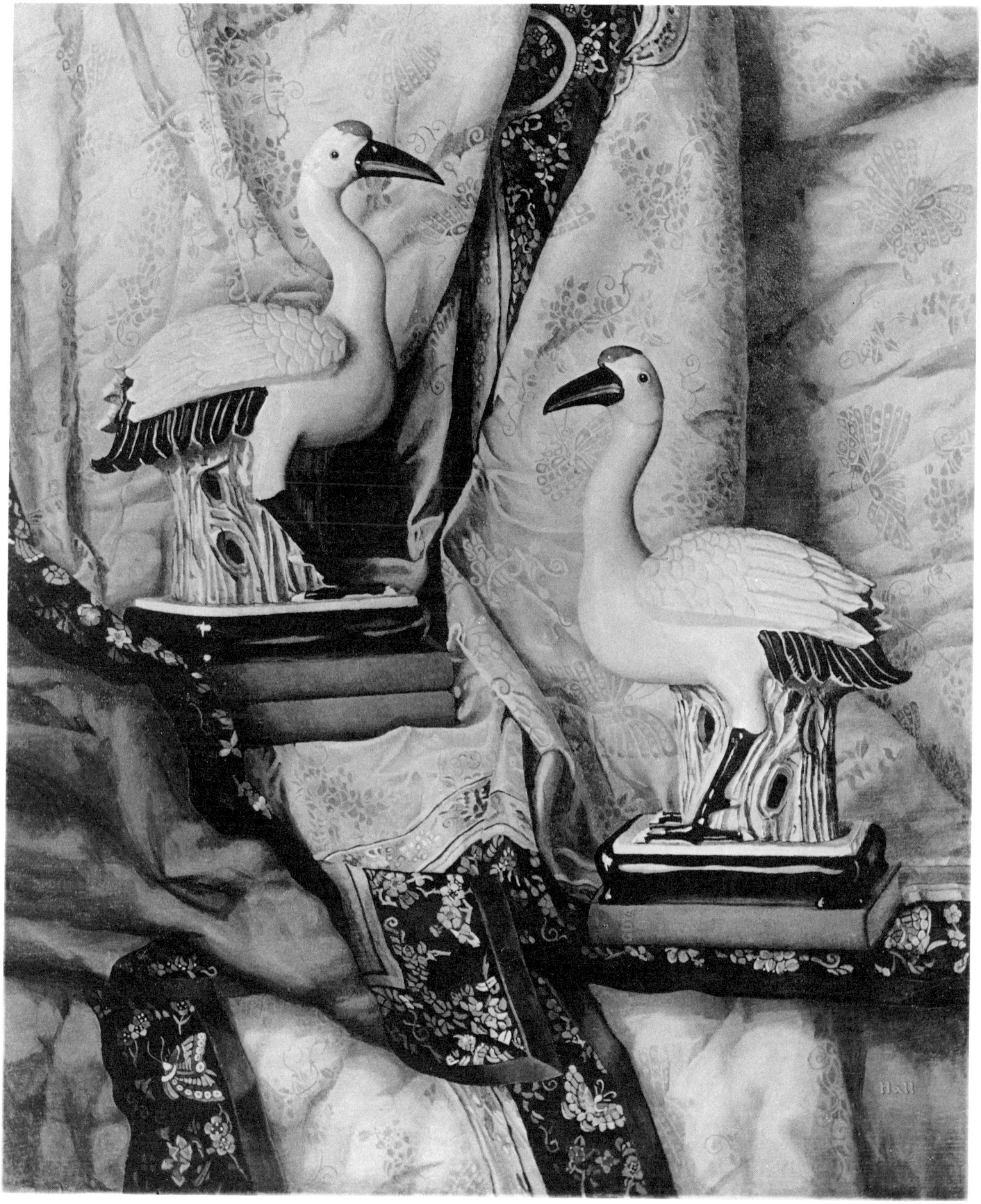

HELEN MACY HALL
Oil on canvas 22½ by 15¾
In the collection of Frederick G. Hall, II.

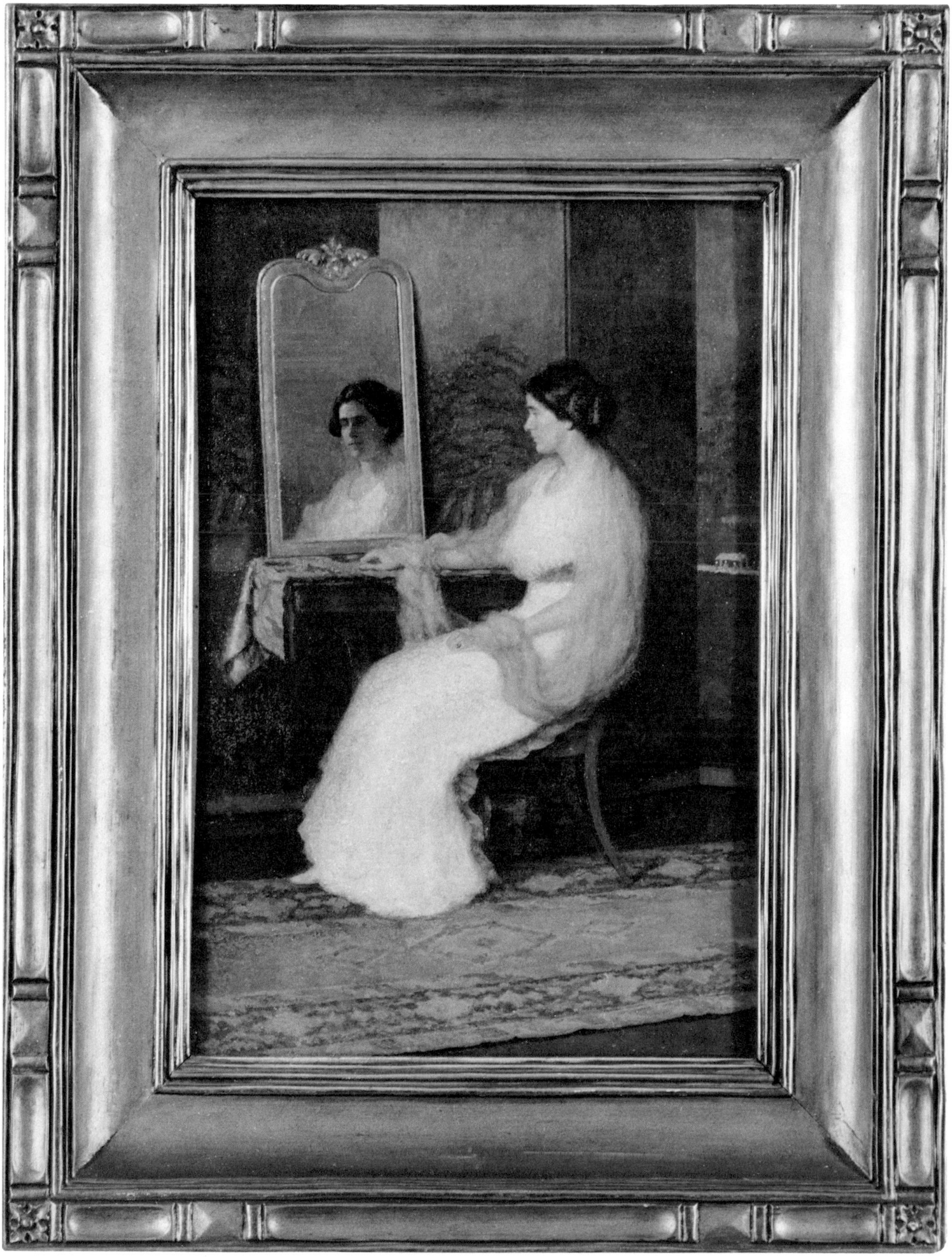

BIBLIOGRAPHY

Bergengren, Ralph. "The Little People of F. G. Hall." *The Print Connoisseur*, v, 4 (October 1925) 326–338.

Castle, Agnes and Egerton. *The Heart of Lady Anne*. With illustrations in color by Ethel Franklin Betts and numerous decorations by Frederick Garrison Hall. New York: Frederick A. Stokes Company, 1905.

Garland, Joseph. *Eastern Point*. Peterborough, New Hampshire: William L. Baughan, 1971.

Hall, Frederick Garrison, Edward Revere Little, and Henry Ware Elliot, Jr. *Harvard Celebrities*. Cambridge, Massachusetts: University Press, 1901.

Heintzelman, Arthur W. "The Etchings of Frederick Garrison Hall." *More Books, The Bulletin of the Boston Public Library*, xxiii, 4 (April 1948) 147–148.

Rihani, Ameen. "The Etchings of Frederick Garrison Hall." *The Print Connoisseur*, i, 3 (March 1921) 218–235.

Sturgis, R. Clipston, Jr. *Bookplates by Frederick Garrison Hall*. Boston: The Troutsdale Press, 1905.

Movies: "Drypoint: A Demonstration."
    A satire on the same subject.

The following issues of *The Bookman* published by Dodd, Mead, & Co. had covers designed by Frederick G. Hall:

December 1901 (Vol. xiv, No. 4)
October 1902 (Vol. xvi, No. 2)
April 1904 (Vol. xix, No. 2)
Christmas 1904 (Vol. xx, No. 4)

The following issues of the Harvard *Lampoon* had covers designed by Frederick G. Hall:

February 3, 1900 (Vol. xxxviii, No. 8)
December 20, 1900 (Vol. xl, No. 6)
February 22, 1901 (Vol. xl, No. 10)
June 21, 1901 (Vol. xli, No. 10)
November 22, 1901 (Vol. xlii, No. 4)
December 19, 1901 (Vol. xlii, No. 6)
March 24, 1902 (Vol. xliii, No. 1)
June 18, 1902 (Vol. xliii, No. 8)
October 31, 1902 (Vol. xliv, No. 2)
December 20, 1902 (Vol. xliv, No. 6)
December 17, 1903 (Vol. xlvi, No. 6)
Cover for the Index to Vol. xlv

APPENDIX A

The Etchings of Frederick Garrison Hall

By Arthur W. Heintzelman

Reprinted from *More Books, The Bulletin of the Boston Public Library*, April 1948

It rarely happens that a graphic artist gains recognition by a limited number of plates. Frederick Garrison Hall through a few well-chosen subjects mastered etching to a degree of international prominence, becoming one of the most talented architectural etchers. He came to the copper plate well prepared in the practice of art in general, having benefited by the thorough instruction of William Paxton, the celebrated Boston painter, and Henri-Paul Royer, the noted French artist.

Hall's progress was direct and determined from the start. With the exception of a few attempts at landscape, several subjects of Gloucester, and a number of finely executed bookplates, there seemed to be no groping, no mixture of styles, or inroads on the methods of others. That he was influenced, as have been most architectural etchers, by the work of Charles Meryon is obvious, but it is surprising that he should have found his vehicle with so little experimentation.

In a sense, Hall was not a realist, for he cared more for the decorative harmony in the arrangement of his values and delicate tones in closely massed lines than he did for the divided contrasts of light and dark. This is particularly true of his French plates, where the surfaces of stone, tile, and other textures are etched with delicacy and feeling. The figures in the original conception of his foregrounds have a certain conventionality, playing an important role in completing the all-power pattern and design. These figures are well drawn, full of expression, and are typical of the environment of each particular subject.

Although Hall produced only a few plates, it seems curious that they did not attract more attention among connoisseurs. The explanation may be in the artist's printing of small editions and his insistence upon the very finest interpretation of the plates. The few impressions that exist are now finding favor among discriminating collectors, who attach due value to their artistic and technical accomplishment.

Subtle treatment of light and shadow, executed with refined technique and excellent draftsmanship, has been used to advantage in "A Scene in Tours." The rich handling of the shadows cast by the intricate Gothic detail upon the white stone façade of this elaborate gate-house has an unusual charm. The cobblestoned entrance to the archway, the adjacent houses, and the unique arrangement of people and workingmen's material in the foreground support the central theme admirably. Everything is sure—correctly and beautifully drawn—yet the detail serves only as a part of the whole.

"La Porte de Guillaume, Rouen" is another interpretation of old French architecture. There is extraordinary solidity and depth in this well-studied composition. Here Hall's natural tastes and knowledge of architectural forms are splendidly recorded in varied technique.

One is fascinated by the artist's choice of subject in the famous seventeenth-century edifice "Église de St. Nicolas du Chardonnet," with its mixture of Gothic and Romanesque. His treatment of the low-peaked tower in comparison to the flying buttresses, tied together with the gabled roof and five-story building, was a test for his entire technical repertoire. Hall has eliminated the houses that existed in the foreground, replacing them with an excavation which in its usual original conception presents a remarkable foundation for his composition. The quality of planes is obtained with much delicate etching, but the whole gives the appearance of oneness and simplicity. The lines, however delicate, are crisp, vigorous, and distinct, with an almost total absence of cross-hatching.

In "La Maison des Cariatides, Dijon" and "Maison des Ambassadeurs, Dijon" an almost perfect mingling of technique and talent may be observed. In suggestion of color, form, and texture they show Hall at the height of his powers. His individuality is fully revealed in these fine studies of the beauties of old architecture, so carefully rendered in detail. Each of the few remaining etchings demands study. The little plate "Old House in Vicenza," the gem of the collection, calls for special mention. This work, the most successful among collectors, was awarded the Nathan I. Bijur Prize by the Brooklyn Society of Etchers, in 1920.

Hall's drawings, which may be classified as studies, were the real preparation for his plates. The pencil studies predict the future accomplishment upon the copper. Back of the drawings is the artist's analytical, alert, and impressionable mind, which acts as a guide to his technical perfection in etching.

It is interesting to make a comparison between the preliminary drawing, the copper plate, and the final impression. That there was careful study from the first conception is evidenced by the faithful reproduction of the drawing to the plate. One might say that, in their particular sort of way, the drawings contain a good part of the thinking process in relation to composition and suggestion of light and shade. They simplify the divergences of uncertainty between the artist and his copper plate; they create an avenue clearing the road of doubts and making way for the direct execution of his intention. It is the complete integration of his forces that places Frederick Garrison Hall among recognized architectural engravers.

Hall was a contributor to the exhibitions of the leading print societies of America. His awards acted only as an incentive for carrying his ideas further. He knew that there was still much to do and learn before he could fulfill his ambition.

The prints shown in the April exhibition constitute the artist's complete etched work, presented to the Print Department by Mrs. Frederick Garrison Hall in memory of the artist, who died two years ago. Students of architecture and fine prints are privileged to study this small but beautiful collection by a man who strove for the highest ideals in art.

APPENDIX B

The Etchings of Frederick Garrison Hall

By Ameen Rihani

Reprinted from *The Print Connoisseur*, March 1921

The art of etching is particularly suited to this age of structural and intellectual passion; and in America it promises to become the national art. The reason for this is not obscured by any of the perverse complexities of modern civilized life, nor is it far to seek. I find it—this may seem odd—in the one word, economy. No, not economy of production, which may yet become an essential need, but economy of expression.

Our structural and intellectual passions, though we may soar in the one to skyscraper heights, pyramidally achieved, and go down in the other to psychoanalytical depths, admit of no frills, no circumlocution. Straight to our goal, or the first move is the first omen of failure. And in etching, the essential thing, the necessary prerequisite is a direct, a natural and forceful, expression. The etcher, of all artists, better responds, in this sense, to our feelings and our needs. Not that poetry is alien to us or that we preclude the light of the imagination; but the Muse, we seem to insist, must come to this modern world in the fashion of the day and make herself one with those who toil and those who only think—or play.

Many attempts have been made, however, and are continually being made to substitute for the essential characteristic of etching, a peculiar technique, a mannerism, agreeable or otherwise; or to conceal the lack of thought, and sometimes thought itself, which is never so forceful as in a direct expression, in a brilliant and meretricious style. Luminous effects, tonalities, aerial vibrations, peculiarities of light and shade, curiosities of decoration or fancy, and such like often have a real artistic value and consequently an artistic appeal; but seldom do they, to my mind, compensate fully for the lack of a direct and forceful expression.

This quality I find in varying degrees in the work of Frederick Garrison Hall, which is of a serious nature, sound and sane, direct—and often forceful—in treatment. He substitutes no makeshift of any kind for diligence and thought. His art will develop, is developing, along lines imbedded in the best traditions. There is already evidence, as I shall show, of a progressive continuity. In other words, there will be no breaks, no violent departures, in his work. It may be rash to make such a prediction, but the reason, considering his achievements and his temperament as reflected therein, seems obvious.

The artist who begins as an architect or who has been a constant student of architecture, which is the case with many American etchers, can never lose reverence for the line and all its varieties and shades of expression. His hand may be trained to the inexorable rigidity of the rule and the compass, but, if he has a poetic feeling, a spirit of artistic creation—an irrepressible desire, in other words, that would always make the conception of his subject ray out of the expression like fire and flame from a living sun—he will soon abandon the compass and rule or have recourse to them only in spacing and composition. And this creative instinct is revealed, not only in some of the etchings of Mr. Hall, but also in his bookplates, particularly those he made more recently, as the *Loring, Sears*, the *Julian Peabody*, and the *Irving Kent Hall* plates, which are beautiful in execution as well as in their artistic conception, their allegorical and poetic conceit.

But through his bookplates and his architectural training, which are but stepping stones, he comes to his art equipped with some of the best principles and handicapped also with a few traditions. The engraver's technique, for instance, which is a kind of tattooing of tones and shades, is quite all right in a bookplate, but it is not adequate, to say the least, in an etching. Mr. Hall is a severe critic of his own work, however, and seldom or never repeats a mistake.

On the other hand, he never seems to lose sight of the fundamental rule, which precludes every makeshift, every shortcut, every trick that has for its purpose the development of a rapid process. *A thought for every line*, we can read this even in the passages that reveal the sureness and facility of a studied carelessness. In other words, he conveys the pleasant impression that he forgets at times the rule. As in *The Cliff*, a delicately executed plate, whose lightness of touch and reticence of line express beautifully the sense of vastness and distance of the open country. An airy something, very enticing, breathes over the scene.

In his architectural plates, we have examples of a fine draftsmanship, a harmony of line, a mastery of detail and composition. But these qualities, excellent as they are, do not completely hide from us the fact that somewhere a spontaneity has been stifled by a rule. Of the two etchings, *House in Vicenza* and *Boston Public Library*, the former is more compact, more direct and sincere. It is freer in execution, and free of those blemishes that betray a hesitating purpose. For while some of the details of the *Boston Public Library* plate are meticulously handled, as the medallions above the frieze, so well drawn, the parenthetical charm of decorative design, the reflections of the buildings across the way in the glass windows, it is nevertheless spoiled for me by the smoke, rising from the engine in the street, and the attempt to balance it with a bit of rococo sky. But Mr. Hall has surpassed himself in his last architectural plate, which illustrates principally the orientation of his purpose as well as the progression of his art. In *Old Houses on the Tiber* he combines, in a sustained effort, the best qualities of the former two. In it also is a florescence of the spontaneous manner, which we shall see better exemplified in the Willow plates.

But his technical skill is revealed at its best in *The Cave*, a strong and forceful expression, direct and free, of that ruggedness in nature which is seldom lacking in the surprise here and there of a balancing grace. Mr. Hall has read rightly this passage in nature's page and has given us a free but faithful representation of it. His sense of decoration serves well to interpret the balancing grace. The three ravens, for instance, in front of the cave, a happy conceit, reflect the magnitude of the scene and bring out to greater effect the cross-hatching, which is neatly, faultlessly done—a technical triumph in itself. One would wish, however, that his needle had not faltered a little in the sky. But he'll get his sky yet, I'm sure. He'll get it, not through any concession to its qualities, obvious or distant or elusive, but by tackling it with a firm purpose and an unwavering hand. And there is a proof of this in *The Deserted Shipyard* and some of his other plates.

On the whole, there is more than technical skill in the etchings of Mr. Hall; there is unquestionably a fine talent in florescence. And as a good example of this florescence, I would call attention particularly to his three Willow plates. The first, *Old Willows*, somewhat tight, reflecting a measured precision, is the seed or the shoot; the second, *Beach and Willows*, revealing a nascent freedom, an articulate charm, is the bud; and *Niles Pond*, with its rare quality of tone, its free and graceful composition, its atmospheric beauty—this is the flower.

How is such development possible? Only through the medium of an artistic heritage and an authentic talent conscientiously tendered and upheld. It is immaterial what masters a true artist may be following in his first stage of development; for soon or late his own individuality will assert itself in an intimate and unmistakable expression. It may not be striking or capricious, this expression; it may be devoid of an arresting mannerism; but so it is sound and sincere and strong, we must heed its claim, acknowledge its virtue, and wish for an increase of its wholesome influence. That is how I feel about an artist like Mr. Hall, who stands for a continuity of noble tradition, who upholds the old ideals, the ever vital ideals of art, without stuffing his ears with cotton or wearing the goggles of an academician.

APPENDIX C

The Little People of F. G. Hall

BY RALPH BERGENGREN

Reprinted from *The Print Connoisseur*, October 1925

SOME YEARS AGO, picking up a book in a library, I came upon a bookplate by Frederick Garrison Hall which remained in memory by virtue of the almost microscopic people he had placed picturesquely in a medieval street. Certain mountebanks anticked on a platform, and a crowd looked on. The distinctive characteristic of the little picture was its combination of fantasy and plausibility—an element of reality added to pictured architecture by something oddly realistic about the crowd and the mountebanks. And this characteristic, without the grotesquerie of the bookplate, I find again in Mr. Hall's latest etchings, in which perception of beauty and authority of technique are given, it seems to me, a peculiar distinction by his selection and treatment of human accessories.

There is, for example, the etching of an old house in Dijon that Mr. Hall has named *La Maison des Cariatides*. Two women have met by chance, one with a bundle and the other with a basket, just outside the old curiosity shop on the ground floor of this house. The house may have been there when Louis XV ruled and ruined in France; but these two gossips certainly were not, and here they serve not only to balance the sculpture of the upper stories and, by contrast of men and women with caryatides, to determine the scale of these ornamental figures, but also to describe the neighborhood in which the old house now stands, and bring pertinently to mind its slow descent from social magnificence to humble utility. The first and simple response of pleasure evoked by the etching comes in part, it may conceivably happen, from the juxtaposition of these humble little people with this ancient architecture of wealth and privilege.

This etching is one of a series of plates—resulting from Mr. Hall's visit to several French towns, with something of Paris, in 1923—that may well delight the expert in such matters by the insight, delicacy, and authority with which the subjects are rendered, and the nonexpert by the less sophisticated enjoyment of looking in his more childlike innocence at the achieved result. In each of these etchings what he has been given to look at, expert or nonexpert, is astonishingly complete in its graphic and beautiful description of an ancient edifice surviving into the present, still alive because it is used or lived in, and, with all its experience upon it, part and parcel with the neighborhood that contains it. To this end many details, not immediately and consciously noticed, must necessarily contribute; and one such detail, I suspect, stands on the feet of these two gossips who (like all the other little people in the plates) are so shrewdly, though unostentatiously, characterized. They add their honest mite to the composite effect of the etching because they have so plausibly met just there and found occasion for that incessant and trivial tongue-wagging which is an endearing characteristic of our common humanity. She with the basket paused a moment, as the turn of her head indicates, to look in the shop window. Time and circumstance have happily brought along her friend with the bundle—and there they are, you see, cheerfully impeding pedestrian traffic on a narrow sidewalk.

So such pleasant episodes happen in Dijon, and elsewhere; and the individualization of their little figures and faces is typical of the dozen human accessories—with one more, leaning out of a second-story window, not much interested in what is going on below but interested enough for want of something more exciting—whose casual presence imparts an everyday reality of continuing life and occupancy to the old house itself. They help explain the special charm of what without them, and without some other details attributable to the etcher's invention and feeling for the windows of an old house as indicative of the life within it, would still be a technically admirable etching of an interesting subject. They are in no way dramatic, as, indeed, would spoil the composite effect to which their plausibility contributes, but they reward the attention that they do not solicit. One might say of them in general that they are delightfully, and even in a quiet way humorously, expressive of the seriousness with which we all take ourselves. The boy who has sat down on some construction work in the foreground—Mr. Hall himself is the construction company that has dug this hole in front of the House of the Caryatides, blithely and rightly closing a street to add interest to an etching—has sat down, in effect, because sitting down just then happened to appeal to him; and the man with a stick, crossing the street to investigate the excavation, is obeying his own normal impulse to see what is down there. Two other good dames just behind our gossips have also fallen to tongue-work, and are not sorry to stop; but the woman behind them with a basket of laundry on her head is naturally impatient, and the young man carrying a live goose has begun to get bored. A fat man is reading a poster on the wall, and there are tiny wrinkles, if you look closely enough, in the back of his neck.

If one went to Dijon one would find this old house facing the end of a street (where Mr. Hall has turned construction company); and one might, if he had the etching along for comparison, discover other details in which the etcher has modified an interesting subject to make a more interesting work of art. It would appear, indeed, that he went into the real estate business, and ejected a modern furniture store from the first floor, reletting the premises to the old curiosity shop that occupies them in the etching. Which is just the kind of a shop that ought to be there. One might discover also that for the good of his composition he climbed a roof and took down a chimney; and perhaps it was his kindly heart and consideration for the people who live there, as well as his regard for his plate, that led him to build them another perfectly good chimney in a different place. In his lease to the old curiosity shop he insisted upon a partial restoration of the ancient entrance.

There is a bridge in Le Mans; a street goes over it, and on this street stand certain old houses. The street goes gently down a hill, and the parapet of the bridge slants accordingly, turning at a right angle where one street meets another. Charmingly picturesque to look at, the houses are still upstanding (though down at the heel) and habitable (though not for me). Smoke comes out of one of the chimneys rising from the peaked roofs, and curtains hang at a lower window, though an upper window lacks sash and panes to protect the dark interior of the garret from wind and weather. Now and again over a long time the needs of contemporary occupants have done this or that to these *French Half-Timbered Houses* (as Mr. Hall names the plate); and if rain gets in through garret windows, it no doubt gets in also through roofs that would be tighter, though much less attractive to prowling etchers, if they were newly slated. In the etching, however, the sun is on them, warming the plaster walls, and making luminous shadows, with subtly uneven edges eloquent of Father Time's persistent enmity to all straight lines, wherever roof, chimney, or woodwork gives opportunity. Quite a number of Mr. Hall's little people are going along the street or have stopped to use the parapet of the bridge as a convenient and comfortable thing to lean on, their tiny figures—whose faces nevertheless have individuality and expression—pleasing the eye with their charmingly ordered rhythm. Yet it is to be noticed that these little people are not too objectively modern, and that in choosing his supernumeraries Mr. Hall has so selected and rendered them that they introduce no disturbing note in the mellow charm of antiquity which is the first single impression that these etchings produce. There may, very likely, be a tall hat in the picture—but it will be in effect an old tall hat. One may know intellectually that all these little people were not there when the subject first attracted the etcher's attention; not so judiciously would twenty or more citizens of Le Mans have arranged themselves. As a matter of fact they came to line the parapet from sketchbooks well filled with studies of street life in old French towns; and this seemingly natural arrangement may easily represent a considerable period of experiment and decision.

Eglise de St. Nicolas du Chardonnet, if one went to Paris to see it, would be found standing across the street from existing houses. One must needs look at it diagonally from along the street to take in the whole elevation, wondering perhaps whether to call it the more Gothic or the more Romanesque, with its square, low-peaked tower on one side, flying buttresses on the other, and a gable roof in which St. Nicolas's architect seems to have started with a determined Gothic intention, and stopped about half-way up. But Mr. Hall, to whom no labor is excessive if it works to the benefit of his etching, has torn down those houses, leaving a fine deep hole, for a workman in the foreground needs a ladder to climb up out of it. Other little workmen are bringing lumber, and perhaps some local realtor has taken over the excavation and is starting to erect a skyscraper. Meantime we who care nothing about real estate improvements in Paris may look directly at the old Church of St. Nicolas, a House of God to which in course of time was added a house for mortals that now has a milk shop on the ground floor, a restaurant on the next, and living quarters at the top.

This foreground treatment seems to have a double intention: decorative, in that it enriches the plate with imaginative ornament, cunningly contrived from the means and method of modern construction work; and realistic, in that it makes this enrichment integral with the subject, and enhances the antiquity of the church by contrast with the modernity of the constructors. One must always remember, however, that the essence of this "realism" is its reticence, and that it remains, even after discovery, modestly subordinate in the first experience of pleasure projected by the unity of the plate. One may go on afterward to further satisfactions in the collaborating details: the solemn procession of celebrants, with crosses and banners, going into the church; the children, watching it, one of them with a hoop; the loiterers outside the milk shop, and the woman looking down from an upper window; horses, workmen, a fellow with a dog and another with an umbrella—the human life of today following its activities with little enough thought of good St. Nicolas and his old church.

There are not so many little people in the etching of the half-timbered *House in Nantes*, standing on the corner where a narrow street meets a wider, and at the far end of the narrower street the scaffolding around a church in process of repair rises in vertical lines above the belfry, pleasing the eye after the fashion of the masts of ships. Two women have stopped to gossip in the middle of the road, and two dogs to rub noses. A sturdy fellow who was coming along with a cart has left it at the curb and stuck his head in at a lower window of the old house. More gossip here—or perhaps a mere matter of business. A fat woman with an umbrella goes ponderously along the narrower street. Mr. Hall himself may have put up the scaffolding around the church tower; and I have reason to believe that he took an upper story off the comparatively modern row of houses along one side of the street. Let the commercially minded rage, and those unfortunates who hold that truth in art means the exact and literal statement of observed fact. There is another truth, and better for the purpose, in the ponderous gait of the fat woman with the umbrella.

It is, after all, what we see unconsciously (though of course it has to be there) that combines with conscious perception to make the first and inclusive impression projected by any work of art. A critic has said that Mr. Hall regards old houses with an "impassioned attention to their idiosyncrasies," and something of the satisfying completeness of these etchings may be attributed to an equally "impassioned" interest in the passing show of life, human and animal, shrewdly seen and utilized for the ensemble of his plates. It is to his artistic credit, for he undoubtedly delights to "do" these useful little people, that they are never too noticeable. One does not consciously see the wrinkles in the fat man's neck —but the etcher enjoyed putting them there, and I suspect that they do their bit.

APPENDIX D

Catalogue of the Memorial Exhibition

Museum of Fine Arts, Boston, March 13 to April 6, 1947

I. PORTRAITS AND SUBJECT PIECES (OIL)

1. John Prentiss
   29½ by 24¼ in.
   Lent by Phillips Academy, Andover

2. Miss Katharine Lane
   19 by 15¼ in.
   Lent by Mrs. Gardner Lane

3. Robert Treat Paine, 2nd
   8¾ by 7¾ in.
   Lent by Mrs. Robert Treat Paine, 2nd

4. Mrs. Charles J. Prescott, Jr.
   37½ by 29½ in.
   Lent by Charles J. Prescott, Jr.

5. Miss Flanagan
   37½ by 29½ in.
   Lent by Mrs. Frederick G. Hall

6. Leah
   71½ by 39½ in.
   Lent by Mrs. Frederick G. Hall

7. Beatrice
   44¼ by 35 in.
   Lent by Mrs. William H. Ames

8. Girl in Blue
   41¾ by 32½ in.
   Lent by Mrs. George Hawley

9. Coquette
   37½ by 29½ in.
   Lent by Mrs. Frederick G. Hall

10. Girl Holding an Apple
    37¼ by 29½ in.
    Lent by Mrs. Frederick G. Hall

11. Girl with a Guitar
    29¾ by 23 in.
    Lent by Mrs. Frederick G. Hall

12. Interior with a Woman Sketching
    29½ by 24½ in.
    Lent by Mrs. Frederick G. Hall

II. STILL LIFES (OIL)

13. Chinese Dancing Figure
    6 by 5 in.
    Lent by Mrs. Frederick G. Hall

14. Kuan-Di, Chinese God of War, no. 1
    19¼ by 15¼ in.
    Lent by Mrs. Frederick G. Hall

15. Kuan-Di, Chinese God of War, no. 2
    19¼ by 15¼ in.
    Lent by Mrs. Frederick G. Hall

16. A Chinese Goddess
    17½ by 15¼ in.
    Lent by Mrs. Frederick G. Hall

17. A Chinese God: Soapstone Figure
    29¼ by 19¼ in.
    Lent by Wright Fabyan
18. The Green Rooster
    29½ by 24½ in.
    Lent by Mrs. Frederick G. Hall
19. The White Rooster, no. 1
    22½ by 18½ in.
    Lent by William T. Aldrich
20. The White Rooster, no. 2
    23½ by 19½ in.
    Lent by William T. Aldrich
21. Horseman (Roof-Tile) with Flying Cranes
    29½ by 23½ in.
    Lent by Mrs. Frederick G. Hall
22. Chinese Figure (Roof-Tile) with a Crane
    29½ by 21½ in.
    Lent by Mrs. N. Penrose Hallowell
23. Chinese Figure (Roof-Tile) with Two Cranes
    29½ by 21½ in.
    Lent by Mrs. George Putnam
24. Roof-Tile: Chinese Horseman, no. 1
    29¼ by 23¼ in.
    Lent by Mrs. Frederick G. Hall
25. Roof-Tile: Chinese Horseman, no. 2
    24½ by 19½ in.
    Lent by Mrs. George Putnam
26. Roof-Tile: Chinese Horseman: "Good News"
    32¾ by 24¾ in.
    Lent by Mrs. Frederick G. Hall
27. The White Crane
    19¼ by 15¼ in.
    Lent by Mrs. Frederick G. Hall
28. Green Mandarin Ducks
    30 by 23 in.
    Lent by Lawrence A. Nowell
29. Harlequin (porcelain)
    27 by 20 in.
    Lent by Mrs. George Lee
30. White Porcelain Boy and Bull's-Eye Mirror
    27½ by 19 in.
    Lent by Mrs. Edward Thaw
31. Norse Fisherman, no. 1 (porcelain)
    29½ by 24½ in.
    Lent by Mr. and Mrs. Arthur Shaw
32. Norse Fisherman, no. 2 (porcelain)
    37¼ by 29¼ in.
    Lent by Mrs. Frederick G. Hall
33. The Duke of Wellington (porcelain)
    17½ by 13½ in.
    Lent by Mrs. Frederick G. Hall
34. General Junot (porcelain)
    18 by 14 in.
    Lent by Mrs. E. Laurence White
35. The Red Dress (porcelain)
    36½ by 36½ in.
    Lent by Edward Ballantine
36. Cleopatra (porcelain)
    17½ by 14½ in.
    Lent by Mrs. Frederick G. Hall
37. White Rabbit (porcelain)
    5½ by 6½ in.
    Lent by R. H. Ives Gammell
38. The Fawn Whippet (porcelain)
    5½ by 6½ in.
    Lent by Mrs. Albert Burrage
39. The White Kid (porcelain)
    7½ by 6½ in.
    Lent by Mrs. C. Nichols Greene
40. The White Whippet (porcelain)
    17¾ by 14½ in.
    Lent by Frederic C. Bartlett
41. Young Bacchus on a Goat (porcelain)
    17¾ by 13½ in.
    Lent by William T. Aldrich

42. Dancing Putto (porcelain)
10 by 8 in.
Lent by Miss Mary O. Bowditch

43. Baigneuse, no. 1 (porcelain)
15¼ by 9½ in.
Lent by Harpo Marx

44. Baigneuse, no. 2 (porcelain)
18 by 13½ in.
Lent by Mrs. Francis T. P. Plimpton

45. Seated Nude (porcelain)
12½ by 12½ in.
Lent by Mrs. Frederick G. Hall

46. The White Giraffe (porcelain)
12½ by 10 in.
Lent by Mrs. Frederick G. Hall

47. Dancing Nude (porcelain)
22¼ by 13¼ in.
Lent by John Thayer Burr

III. ETCHINGS

48. Old Willows
Lent by Mrs. Frederick G. Hall

49. The Public Library, Boston
Lent by Mrs. Frederick G. Hall

50. Beach and Willows
Lent by Doll & Richards, Inc.

51. Old Houses on the Tiber
Lent by Mrs. Frederick G. Hall

52. House in Oleron
Lent by Mrs. Frederick G. Hall

53. House in Vicenza
Lent by Mrs. Frederick G. Hall

54. Ancient Doorway, Nevers
Lent by Mrs. Frederick G. Hall

55. Hotel Moret
Lent by Mrs. Frederick G. Hall

56. Old French Half-timbered Houses—Le Mans
Lent by Mrs. Frederick G. Hall

57. A House in Nantes
Lent by Mrs. Frederick G. Hall

58. Old Timer
Lent by Doll & Richards, Inc.

59. The Deserted Shipyard
Lent by Doll & Richards, Inc.

60. Église de St. Nicolas du Chardonnet
Lent by Mrs. Frederick G. Hall

61. Little French Market
Lent by Mrs. Frederick G. Hall

62. La Maison des Ambassadeurs, Dijon
Lent by Mrs. Frederick G. Hall

63. La Maison des Cariatides
Lent by Mrs. Frederick G. Hall

64. A Scene in Tours
Lent by Mrs. Frederick G. Hall

65. Tour Goguin
Lent by Mrs. Frederick G. Hall

66. Rouen-Porte de Guillaume
Lent by Mrs. Frederick G. Hall

67. Gateway, Rotterdam
Lent by Mrs. Frederick G. Hall

68. Diana
M.F.A., Horatio G. Curtis Fund

69. Dijon-Eglise de Notre Dame
Lent by Mrs. Frederick G. Hall

BOOKPLATES

70. William Truman Aldrich; Dorothea Davenport Aldrich
Gift of Mrs. Frederick G. Hall

71. Shepherd Stevens
Gift of Mrs. Frederick G. Hall

72. Eleanor Cochrane Sears
Gift of Mrs. Frederick G. Hall

73. Irving Kent Hall; Helen Macy Hall
Gift of Mrs. Frederick G. Hall

IV. DRAWINGS

74. Church of St. Mary Woolnoth, London
    Lent by Arthur W. Heintzelman

75. Gateway, Rotterdam
    Lent by Miss Marion L. Hunt

76. Rouen-Porte de Guillaume
    Lent by Mrs. Frederick G. Hall

77. Tour Goguin
    Lent by Mrs. Frederick G. Hall

78. La Maison des Cariatides
    Lent by Thomas Taylor, Jr.

79. Église de St. Nicolas du Chardonnet
    Lent by Thomas Taylor, Jr.

80. Portrait of Robert Treat Paine, 2nd
    Lent by Mrs. Thomas Metcalf

81. Head of a girl, facing front
    Lent by Mrs. Frederick G. Hall

82. Head of a woman, facing left
    Lent by Mrs. Frederick G. Hall

83. Head of a woman, profile to right
    Lent by Mrs. Frederick G. Hall

84. Head of a woman, looking down
    Lent by Mrs. Frederick G. Hall

85. Head of a girl, with boyish hair cut
    Lent by Mrs. Frederick G. Hall

86. A nude model, standing
    Lent by Mrs. Frederick G. Hall

Index of Prints

The first number denotes the page of the catalogue entry. Succeeding numbers denote references.

Ancient Doorway, Nevers, 46
Beach and Willows, 24, 117
Boston Public Library, 38, 116
By the Pond, 32
The Cave, 20, 116
The Cliff, 30, 116
The Deserted Shipyard, 34, 117
Diana, 76
Dijon, Eglise de Notre Dame, plates 1 and 2, 72; plate 3, 74, 11
Eglise de St. Nicolas du Chardonnet, 58, 7, 114, 120
Entrance to Pennsylvania Station, 42, 7
Gateway, Rotterdam, 70
Hotel Moret, 50
House in Nantes, 52, 121
House in Oleron, 44
House in Vicenza, 40, 114, 116

Italian Villa, 42, 7
Little French Market, 64
Maison des Ambassadeurs, Dijon, 56, 114
La Maison des Cariatides, Dijon, 60, 114, 118
Niles Pond, 26, 117
Old French Half-Timbered Houses, Le Mans, 48, 120
Old Houses on the Tiber, 42, 116
Old Timer, 54
Old Willow, 28
Old Willows, 22, 117
La Pensionnaire Americaine, 36
Prescott, Mrs. Charles J., Jr., 78
The Rocky Field, 16
Rouen, Porte de Guillaume, 68, 114
Salem Cedar, 18
A Scene in Tours, 66, 113
Tour Goguin, 62

Index of Bookplates

Aldrich, William Truman, and Dorothea Davenport Aldrich, 83
Allen, Herbert Spencer, 83
Ames, Anna C., Memorial Scholarship, 83
Ames, Susan Evelyn, 83
Ames, Oakes, 84
Baker, Alfred Talbot, 84
Brown, Archibald Manning, 84
Bulkley, Robert Johns, 84
Chatman, Anna Ray, 85
Forbes, Helen Cady, 85
Fuller, Benjamin Apthorp Gould, 85
Fuller, Robert Gorham, 85

Glasgow, William H., 86
Graves, John Raynor, 86
Green, Walton Atwater, 86
Greenough, David Stoddard, 86
H., M.G., 87
Hall, Frederick Garrison, 87
Hall, Irving Kent, 87
Hall, Irving Kent, and Helen Macy Hall, 88
Harvard University, Nelson Robinson Fund, 88
Haughton, Alison, 88
Hooper, Parker Morse, 88
Jackson, Isaac, 89
Jones, Lillian Durham, 89

Junkin, Joseph de Forest, Jr., 89
Lane, Katharine Ward, 89
Little, Clarence Cook, 90
Loring, Susan M., 90
Loring, William Caleb, 90
Mott, Lawrence, 90
Nowell, George M., and Anna Lee Ames Nowell, 91
Page, Louis Coues, 91
Paxton, William McGregor, 91
Peabody, Julian, 91
Roelvink, Herman Christiaan Juriaan, 92
Schlesinger, Armin A., 92

Scott, Clement, 92
Sears, Eleanor Cochrane, 92
Smith, Caroline Hooper, 93
Sperry, Charles Stillman, 93
Stevens, Shepherd, 93
Straus, Herbert Nathan, 94
Sturgis, Richard Clipston, Jr., 94
Truesdell, Amy Ivers, 94
Tuckerman, Walter Rupert, 94
Warner, Langdon, 95
White, Herbert Hill, 95
Yule, Harriet Head, 95
Zanetti, Carlos Alberto, 95

General Index

Ames, Evelyn, *see* Hall, Evelyn Ames
The Bookman, 8; cover reproduced, 105
Boston, 7, 8, 10, 11, 12
Boston Public Library, 9, 12, 113
Dijon, France, 118, 119
Endicott, William, 13, 14
France, 11, 118
French plates, 113, 114, 118–121
Gloucester, Massachusetts, 8, 11, 13, 14, 113
Hall, Ariel Perry (2nd wife of F.G.H.), 9, 12, 114; article by, 10–12
Hall, Evelyn Ames (1st wife of F.G.H.), 11, 14
Hall, Frederick Garrison
  Ancestry, 10
  Architecture, interest in, 8, 10, 114–116
  Awards: Nathan I. Bijur Prize, 40; Alice Brinton Gold Medal, 64; Alice McFadden Eyre Gold Medal, 42; Honorable Mention, 58, 66; Charles M. Lea Prize, 60; Logan Prize, 60; Silver Medal, Sesqui-centennial International Exposition, 56; Jennie Sesnan Gold Medal, 42
  Bookplates, 8, 10, 82, 116; reproduced, 83–95
  Drawing, 11, 114; drawings reproduced, 99, 101
  Education, 10, 11, 113
  Etching, attitude toward, 14
  Homes, 10, 11, 14
  Humor, sense of, 12, 13
  Magazine covers, 8; covers reproduced, 103, 105
  Music, interest in, 10, 11, 14; harp, 11
  Painting, 8, 12; paintings reproduced, 107, 109
  Studios, 11, 13; photograph, 80
  Theatre, interest in, 11
  Travel, 11
Hall, Irving Kent, 10
Harvard University, 8, 10
Harvard *Lampoon*, editor of, 10; covers for, 8, 103
Heintzelman, Arthur W., 7; article by, 113–114
Le Mans, France, 119–120
Marx, Harpo, 11, 14
Meryon, Charles, influence of, 11, 113
Museum of Fine Arts, Boston, 9, 12, 13, 14
National Academy of Design, 12; painting of F.G.H., 6
Paris, 11, 12, 118, 120
Paxton, William McGregor, 10, 113
Perry, Ariel Wellington, *see* Hall, Ariel P.
Print Connoisseur, The, 7; articles from, 115–117, 118–121
Rossiter, Henry P., 9; article by, 13–14

PERSONS AND PLACES MENTIONED ONLY

Academie Julien, 11
Ames, Oliver, 11
Art Institute of Chicago, 12
Attleboro, Massachusetts, 12
Baltimore, Maryland, 10
Benson, Frank, 13
Bibliothèque Nationale, 8, 12
Boston Athenæum, 8
Boston Symphony, 11

Braque, Georges, 10
Brooklyn, New York, 7
Brooklyn Society of Etchers, 114
Chicago, 7
Coffee House, 12
Cole, Timothy, 13
Contee family, 10
Copley Society, 7
Curtis Institute, 12

Dilling, Mildred, 11
Dodd, Meade & Co., 8
Doll & Richards, 7
Duvall family, 10
Eastern Point, 11
England, 11
Fendall, Josias, 10
Florence, Italy, 12
Garrison family, 10
Guild of Boston Artists, 7
Hall, Garrison K., 7
Hall, Rev. Henry, 10
Hall, Joseph Thomas, 10
Hall, Myra Garrison, 10
Harvard Club of New York, 12
Hitchings, Sinclair, 8
Holland, 11
Huntington, Anna Vaughn Hyatt, 8
Italy, 11
Joan of Arc, 8
Keith, Freeman, 9
Kent, Joseph, 10
Library of Congress, 12
Louis XV, 118
Maryland, 10
Matisse, Henri, 10
Miller, Alice Duer, 11

New York, 8, 12
North Easton, Massachusetts, 11
Orcutt, William Dana, 10
Peckham, John, 9
Peltz, Karin, 9
Perry, Clara Brigham, 12
Perry, Everett Inwood, 12
Philadelphia, 7, 12
Picasso, Pablo, 10
Players Club, The, 12
Roth, Ernest D., 8
Royal Italian Committee on Arts
    Acquisition, 8
Royer, Henri-Paul, 113
St. Botolph Club, 7, 11
Sayre, Eleanor, 9
Smith College, 12
Sorbonne, 12
Sturgis, Richard Clipston, 8
Swenson, Paul, 8
Uffizi Gallery, 8, 12
University Press, Cambridge, 10
Washington, D.C., 12
Whitehill, Walter Muir, 8
Wiggin Collection, 12
Young, Roland, 11
Zighera, Bernard, 11

Frederick Garrison Hall: Etchings, Bookplates, Designs,
has been designed and set in type by The Stinehour Press, Lunenburg, Vermont.
Reproductions, in 300-line-screen photo-offset lithography, are by
The Meriden Gravure Company, Meriden, Connecticut, which has printed the book
in an edition of five hundred copies.
The type face is Monotype Bell, the paper Mohawk Superfine.

This is copy no.

233

here signed by the author

Elton W. Hall